THE SECRET LIFE OF
MOTHER WONDERFUL

The Secret Life of

MOTHER WONDERFUL

Myra Chanin

BEAUFORT BOOKS, INC.
New York   Toronto

Library of Congress Cataloging in Publication Data

Chanin, Myra.
  The secret life of Mother Wonderful.
  I. Title.
PN6162.C47   813'.54   80-22904
ISBN 0-8253-0021-5

Published in the United States by Beaufort Books, Inc.
Published simultaneously in Canada by Nelson, Foster and Scott Ltd.

Designer: Ellen LoGiudice

Printed in the U.S.A.
First Edition

10 9 8 7 6 5 4 3 2 1

For
(in alphabetical order)
Alvin Chanin
Barney Dlin
Paul Vinicoff

They know why.

TABLE OF CONTENTS

CAST OF CHARACTERS

I am MOTHER WONDERFUL, a Frog Princess, a gifted daughter who never did anything right. Cursed with a low bullshit tolerance, unreceptive to dogma, I was born with defective "good daughter" genes and took the road that was loaded with ravines.

At 30 I was a failure. Unmarried. Unemployed. A triple college dropout. My jobs were never in the same league as my Stanford-Binet Scores. My specialty was collecting unemployment compensation. I may have set a world record by collecting for 75 weeks.

At 41 I began to bake cakes as Mother Wonderful. I thought I was on my way to Splitsville and I knew I would need money. When my marriage stabilized I gave up baking and began to write and no one is more surprised than I to find myself 46 and a published author.

FATHER WONDERFUL, my husband Alvin, is a lawyer, C.P.A., record producer, and the owner of a fleet of small boats, none of them seaworthy. He is the only man I've ever met either courageous or insensitive enough to survive 15 years married to me. My striving for perfection bewilders him. He thinks he's already perfect. Our slightly different views of his character keep our relationship vital, challenging, and frequently on the rocks.

I have dragged him from one wonder-working headshrinker to the next looking for incantations to cure his emotional constipation, and each time I expect instant results. "Even the Miracle of the Bells took a week!" he once complained. He also supplies me with many of my best one-liners.

Our son STEVEN, a perverse and analytical 12-year-old, is living proof that God heard my mother's curses and gave me a child who is exactly like me. My mother should have been more precise in her selection of words. I would have had more grief if she had wished a child on me who resembled her.

SPOT, the world's dumbest dog, is a kinky hound, inclined to mate in traffic, who pursues bitches, squirrels, and my son's dearest friend Eddie Porter with the same unbridled lust. Part desert dog (his skeleton), part jackal (his markings), part camel (his bladder), Spot is a full-blooded Canaan, an upstart Israeli breed whose longing for legitimacy is ignored by the American Kennel Club.

BARON POTTSTOWN, the muse of articles, is a jealous genius and my dearest friend. He's an architect whose artistic standards are far more elegant than his clients, and who dreams of meeting a perfect patron at one of the many charity galas he attends. Baron's idea of a perfect client is some 98-year-old widow with more inheritance than sight, too weak-eyed to decipher the bills for Carerra marble. Baron's real mission on earth, however, is to act as my substitute mother and keep me from enjoying too much pleasure from even minor success. Any mention of my name in the media is always followed by a letter from him in which I am addressed as "occupant."

BECKY YOUNG, a Philadelphia photographer, changed my life when she made my naked body into a work of art. Thanks to her I discovered that the torso I had always considered third-rate was actually only second-rate. If I had only met her while I was a teen-ager, I might be ruler of the world today.

My MOTHER (Sylvia, Tsuni, Sonya) was a perfect daughter who hoped I would follow in her footsteps, which led right into my grandmother's grave. Tsuni fantasizes about lying comatose for a decade sustained by the best respirators that money can rent. When she is not denying herself pleasure in order to secure the funds for her dream, she occupies herself with futilely attempting to transform me into my cousin Harriet's double.

HARRIET, daughter of Della, my aunt, wife of doctor, mother of medical students, is a 50-year-old drudge who looks 65. Harriet wins cleaning competitions with her maid. Despite agonizing attacks of ulcerative colitis, Harriet washes her own floors and drives Della to Reading, only 90 miles away, whenever Della needs a new pair of panty hose. Stockings cost a quarter less in Reading and Della doesn't like to waste her own money. She prefers to waste Harriet's time and gasoline.

BENNY, my father-in-law, is a swinging Miami Beach widower who became a social success at the age of 72. Benny has conquered angina with the aid of the latest dance steps and Renate, a widow after whose estate he lusts.

THE SECRET LIFE OF MOTHER
WONDERFUL

Nuclear Refugee

I am a white-knuckle flyer with no confidence in the laws of aerodynamics. Every second I spend in midair is a flight against fear. In the lounge I carefully examine the faces of my fellow passengers. Do any look doomed? Just let one of those poor souls on the Whisperjet with you and it's curtains for everyone.

Even minor variations in the whine of the engines spur me into 40 minutes of prayer. I am unnerved by turbulence, suspicious of seat belts. I only wear clothing with preservative clout. Among the clouds, my sole comfort is the presence of my husband Alvin in the seat beside mine. No motor would dare to fail a man with such a vile temper.

This past winter when my 11-year-old-son Steven begged me to take him skiing over Spring vacation, the decline of the dollar made an excursion to the Alps unthinkable. I found other excuses to avoid the Rockies. Aspen was corrupt. Vail was overcrowded. Big Sky was primitive, Sun Valley remote. The same week Steven was off, my neighbors, Paul Bockenhauer and Peter Arfaa, were taking their kids skiing at Grey Rocks, a family resort above Montreal with a third-rate mountain and downright lousy food, petty shortcomings when compared with the area's most stellar attraction. I could get there without boarding an iron bird.

Peter and Paul were driving up in a rented van and offered to transport our luggage. Steven and I would travel to Canada by train. Alvin was too busy to come along. His

favorite clients, five unemployed singers, were once more
launching themselves toward superstardom with my savings
as their fuel. Alvin predicts that his share of this group's
future earnings will make us rich beyond our wildest
dreams. I have a less sentimental view of entertainers. I
know he will be repaid with ingratitude.

Alvin's love of music is an unrequited passion. Melodies
boycott his vocal chords. Lyrics trip scrambled through his
lips. Can a partially deaf lawyer find happiness as a Disco
Czar? The annals of music are filled with stranger tales.
Beethovan was deaf as a post and still composed those
Golden Oldies. Alvin's just as persistent as Beethoven and
only half as deaf. Imagine the Hot 100 blaring over giant
speakers hour after hour. In such brutal working conditions,
Alvin's 42 percent hearing loss is a real blessing.

The first record Alvin ever invested in, "The Hava Na-
gilla Hustle," was a musical miscegenation that taught him
how to handle failure. Now, he always asks my opinion
before he signs any checks. A youth misspent with an embit-
tered saxophone player turned me into a musical Cassandra
with a gift of prophecy but only for flops. Alvin made me
promise to review the rhythm tracks over the long-distance
telephone. His standing as a guru depends on how accurately he repeats my critiques.

Alvin drove me and Steven to the train on his way to the
studio. With his khaki shirt open to his navel and his disco
chain pressing against the gray hair on his chest, Alvin
looked like a recently-divorced dentist. No time for tender
farewells. He kissed and ran. The bass guitarist and the
drummer had already come to blows and Alvin was needed
to conduct the peace negotiations. Steven immediately
realized I had lied to him about the train. The Montrealer
was a far cry from the Orient Express. The food in the din-

ing car saved the day. Steven loved it. Pure swill.

The first selection on the slopes of Grey Rocks separated the moms from the boys. I skied with sensible adults who cared about survival, not sport. Steven raced down ravines with the Kamikaze Cadets and never came near my side of the hill, not even to ride the lifts. On previous ski vacations, cries of "Chicken! Chick-en!" from the heavens always made me wonder if God was urging me to ski more aggressively or merely announcing the dinner menu.

On Wednesday afternoon, I first heard about trouble at Three Mile Island. I called Alvin and he told me not to worry. Alvin's instincts are usually infallible. He wrote the manual on self-preservation. He managed to spend the Korean War two-finger typing morning reports at Fort Belvoir while his original outfit (cadre) all dodged bullets at the front.

On Thursday the headlines were more menacing, but Alvin was still blasé.

"Why are they venting radiation?" I asked him. "Why are they dumping radioactive water in the Susquehanna?" Ever since Nixon's fall I have trouble taking the bureaucracy at face value.

"Yellow journalism," Alvin mumbled. "They'll do anything to sell newspapers."

"But I heard this on the TV," I replied. Cronkite doesn't lie.

More pressing problems occupied Alvin. Behind him, drums and cymbals clashed 128 times every minute. "What do you think of the rhythm track?" he asked with baited breath.

It needed some high pitched sounds to loosen it up. "Add a tambourine or a flute or vibes," I suggested. "What about the bubble?"

"Bubbles are Lawrence Welk's thing. They'll never go in a disco!" Have you ever tried to communicate with anyone so nuts?

I couldn't believe my ears. "Listen, Alvin," I interrupted. "I'm really worried. Things don't sound good."

"What doesn't sound good?" he screamed. "Before you left you told me you loved this arrangement!" He insisted I was overreacting to the possible destruction of the Middle Atlantic States. His calm in the face of my terror made me wonder which one of us should be committed.

I called Philadelphia later that night to get a second opinion and interrupted Baron Pottstown in the middle of pumping iron. Baron lifts weights to diffuse his rage when his architectural clients ignore his bills. The rent was almost due and he was in no mood to offer comfort when he didn't know how long he would have a roof over his head. "I can't believe you're wasting money on long-distance calls to talk about such nonsense," he snapped. "Do you really expect to live forever?"

"Just long enough to be seduced by fame," I replied. Posthumous glory did not motivate me. I just wanted to get on the talk shows.

On Saturday morning, while everyone else raced down the beginners' hill, I sat in front of the TV in the lodge lobby and watched the same dismal report seven times. Finally, at 11, I walked down to the cocktail lounge for one last drink with my class. Tony was waiting at our table. He was a brand new skier who had pushed himself into our advanced class. I had really disliked him until the previous evening when he let down his hair. Underneath his aggressive New York exterior, he was a victim of chic morality. His open marriage had closed the day his wife revealed that other bodies turned her on more than his did. Tony's repressed machismo could only sustain her infidelities until she began to enjoy them.

"I couldn't race. I have an abscess," Tony mumbled and pointed at his jaw. "As soon as I finish this drink I'm leaving for town to see if I can get a druggist to sell me some antibiotics."

I always carry a pharmacy when I travel with Steven. When I don't have the cure, he always gets the affliction. I offered Tony my penicillin and he walked back to my room with me to get it.

After he had swallowed two pills and we were returning to the bar, Tony casually asked me where I lived. When he heard I came from Philadelphia, he stopped and earnestly clutched my hand. "Listen to me," he whispered, his dark eyes staring into my very soul. "Don't go back. The situation at the reactor is much worse than they're letting on."

"Oh, my God!" I cried. My heart told me that Tony was telling the truth. Hadn't I learned during the Watergate hearings that the entire bureaucracy was staffed with liars?

"I just spoke to a guy I went to Law School with who works for the Agency. The instruments in the reactor are all inoperative. If there's a meltdown everything in a 500 mile radius will go. New York. Washington. Baltimore . . ."

"Philadelphia!" I wailed. "But the evacuation plans . . ."

"What evacuation plans?" Tony took out a wad of bills and asked a less rhetorical question. "How much do I owe you for the antibiotics?"

I couldn't take money from my heavenly messenger, this Noah who had pulled me from a fiery furnace. "Oh, forget it. You've already paid me. You may have saved my life!" I replied melodramatically. Could you expect any less from a woman who had spent her entire adolescence in the dark with Warner Brothers?

Continuing to confuse biblical allusions, I had decided that Steven and I (like Shadrach and Meshach) were the two by two. We had to convince Abednego to stop dancing the Hustle to his doom and board the ark with us.

Tony gave my his home telephone number. His answering service would forward all messages. We kissed goodbye. He left for New York to pick up his wife and children. The crisis had convinced Anita to re-evaluate Tony's charms. She and the children were driving to safety with him . . . somewhere in Michigan.

I felt as if I were having a nightmare, but I couldn't manage to wake up. I walked back to the hotel to find my traveling companions. After I shared Tony's inside dope with Peter and Paul, I was no longer a lone hysteric. All three of us frantically dialed home. To no avail. Our next of kin were all out, blissfully soaking up gamma rays.

Right before lunch, Jeanne, Paul's wife, answered the phone. She had no idea the situation was so desperate. We appointed her coordinator. She was to contact the others and prepare to evacuate. We would call again when we reached Montreal.

We all threw our possessions in the back of the van. Paul drove south in silence. At 4:30 we arrived in Montreal, hurried down to the bank of telephones in the waiting room of the train station and called home again.

Good news! Jeanne and Anne announced that the bubble appeared to be stabilizing. The chances of a meltdown had decreased. Alvin was delighted that I sounded rational once more. He wasn't sure I had been wrong, but when I returned to Philadelphia the following morning, we could discuss whether to stay or leave.

We all had a snack and then Peter, Paul and their children climbed into the van and drove toward home. Steven and I returned to the waiting room. I bought apples and cheese to sustain me on the long journey home. Steven dropped a quarter in one of the rental TV's. He sat down to watch a horror film. The horror film was displaced by a horror news report. The bubble was getting bigger and nobody knew how to reduce it!

I cancelled our train reservations and called Alvin at the studio. "Shu-bee-doo-bee-doo-bee-doo-bee-dooo-ooo . . . " the group serenaded me while I pleaded with Alvin to come to his senses.

"I can't leave now," he hissed, embarrassed by my perpetual phone calls. "We're in the middle of cutting background vocals. Stop overreacting, Myra! I hear reports here too, and things just aren't that bad!"

"I don't know what they're telling you, but I just heard that the bubble could blow at any minute! I'm not coming home, and I'm not sending Steven home either! You're not going to kill us!" I had reached the end of my patience. I could not believe I had married such a fool. "The Jews in Poland wouldn't believe the extermination camps existed either, not even after they were confronted with eyewitness reports. Are you really telling me that you believe that double talk on TV? Remember Alvin, those who cannot remember history are doomed to repeat it!" I snapped, quoting Santayana to him.

Alvin, however, quoted me. "We're adding tambourines and vibes, just like you said. How do the background vocals sound now?"

"Tom is flat!" I screamed. "Get out of there!"

"I can't!" he screamed back. "They need me."

"What for? You can't tell a C from an F sharp!"

"I have to sign the checks," he explained. "Call me later when you get a hotel and let me know where you're staying!" He slammed down the phone without even saying good-bye.

Steven and I had only one change of underwear with us. All our clothing was driving toward Albany in Paul's van. Even more unnerving was the realization that my checkbook and all my credit cards were stashed amid my dirty clothes. I was stranded, a thousand miles from home, with only 50 bucks in traveler's checks.

I could have borne my exile with as much dignity as the Duke of Windsor if I were able to imitate his lifestyle. Being cut off from family and friends was depressing enough, but poverty at my age was just unbearable. My available cash would barely pay for breakfast at the Queen Elizabeth Hotel. I inquired at the information desk about less expensive digs.

"The LaSalle Hotel is real nice," the woman who manned the booth assured me. "It used to be the top hotel in town."

Maybe in '04. In 1979, the LaSalle was a haven for displaced persons, me and 700 boat people.

Our room had crimson walls. The furniture was scarred with cigarette burns. The window didn't shut at all, a blessing in disguise, because we couldn't figure out how to turn down the heat. Only one channel on the TV worked, the one with the terrible news. I called Alvin to let him know where I was and then wallowed in destructive fantasies.

After the 12 o'clock news I called him at the studio for the last time and turned on the guilt machine. I put Steven on the phone. He pulled out all the stops. "I love you, Dad," he whispered. "I don't want to be an orphan. I don't want to visit a communal grave when I need advice about making out."

"Save yourself before it's too late," I pleaded.

"Party tonight. Get down and party tonight!" the background vocals pleaded. As usual the lead singer was slightly flat.

Steven and I ate the bruised apples and stale cheese for dinner, and finally fell asleep at one A.M. with all the lights in the room still on. At four A.M. the phone rang. I jumped out of bed to answer it. Alvin was on the other end with the most terrifying news I had heard all week. He had called Air Canada and arranged for Steven and me to catch the 9 A.M. flight to Miami that morning.

Alvin's father lives in Miami Beach. He would meet us at the airport. Alvin would join us beneath the sheltering palms as quickly as he could.

Fly! Fly to Miami Beach! Fate had certainly dumped a load of shit on me. I was faced with a real dilemma. I had to choose between two forms of certain death. Should I be burned to a crisp in a nuclear meltdown or should I meet my maker after a plane crash in the Okefenokee swamps. Which was worse—the Nukes, or flying without any of my props? The Nukes won.

Steven was delighted to extend his spring vacation with a week in Florida. He did not understand my look of un-abashed horror. How could I admit to a child who admired my intellectual courage that his mother is a masochistic coward who must undergo complicated rituals before she can force her body into the Wild Blue Yonder?

I need a week to convince myself that I will die of a heart attack while eating quenelles at Lutèce. I always wear the same flying togs—a purple turtleneck and herringbone tweed slacks that helped me survive a TAP charter on which the Latin mechanics could not manage to hook up the overhead reading lamps to the consoles of the seats under them. The most important prop is a filthy plastic baggie filled with broken jewelry—the silver skeleton of a cheap lavaliere and some blue and white beads from a bracelet that was reputed to avert the evil eye. Heap strong medicine. Where were they? Under my nighties at home.

Under normal circumstances I sip Perrier at parties. The only pills I ever swallow are capsules of Vitamin C. Threaten me with cloudtime and I become a drunken dope fiend who attempts to combine Dramamine, valium, and vodka into a magic elixir that will permit the taker to fly to her destination in a completely comatose state. The formula is still imperfect. One kink has to be ironed out. The dosage always knocks me out, but never in midair—only after I am back on solid ground.

I could not guzzle Bloody Marys at dawn in front of an impressionable child, nor hustle tranquilizers from perfect strangers. Had my daily jogs strenthened my cardiovascular system enough so that it could endure three hours of intense anxiety without charms, pills, booze, or Alvin?

I felt better when I saw our plane was a 747, the only aircraft in which I have the slightest confidence. It was only one quarter full which lowered my odds of tagging along when some stranger's number was up. My fellow passengers were mostly Orthodox Jews. I hoped they were not chosen people. Steven and I played canasta all the way to Miami. He won every game. I was too busy concentrating all my psychic powers on keeping the motors operative to remember what discards he needed to go out.

After 230 silent repetitions of "The Lord is my Shepherd . . . " the signal to extinguish all cigarettes lifted my heart. The descent, which frightens sensible folks, fills me with joy. It means the end of my terror, one way or another.

Bell Telephone declared an additional dividend that quarter. The wires between Miami Beach and Philadelphia really buzzed. Alvin never did fly down to join me. By Monday the nuclear threat seemed inconsequential to him.

On Tuesday morning I called Tony's answering service and asked them to contact Michigan for me and get the true dope. He was in his Manhattan office. His reconciliation had collapsed along with the bubble. Tony agreed. There was nothing to worry about. It was time to go home.

There were no train reservations, so I booked seats on the noon flight. Statistically, fewer aircraft crash during daylight hours. I stole my father-in-law's last three valium pills and was driven to the airport in a state of grace. As usual, the pills stopped working during the take-off. I drank two Bloody Marys before lunch. Steven didn't help matters much. He just couldn't get it through his head that if I were interested in hearing all the gory details of the midair disasters in *Airport* and *Son of Airport* I would have gone to see the films with him.

Two hours later I collapsed into the arms of my beloved, grateful to have been spared a B-movie death. No appointment in Samarra for me that round. I had not, after all, fled from a rampant reactor only to meet my end in a airline calamity.

My feelings of relief activated the V and V (valium and vodka). I slept all the way home from the airport. I don't remember much after that. Alvin says I passed out until dinnertime.

Up in the sky twice without my jujubeads and alive to tell the tale! Did that triumph teach me how silly it was to take a filthy plastic bag filled with broken jewelry in the bottom of my reticule every time we went on vacation?

It did indeed. I have rehoused my charms in a new macramé amulet which looks wonderful on my purple turtleneck. I really do understand that air currents keep planes aloft. I just wear the necklace for insurance, in case the forces of gravity and inertia should suddenly run amuck.

They Walk By Night

I hate my dog Spot, a kinky hound, inclined to mate in traffic, who chases after bitches, squirrels, and Eddie Porter (my son's dearest friend) with the same unbridled lust. Part desert dog (his body), part jackal (his markings), part camel (his bladder), Padre Hiram Spot is a full-blooded Canaan. Canaans are an upstart Israeli breed whose presumptions of legitimacy are ignored by the American Kennel Club.

My husband Alvin and I learned about Canaans at a cocktail party from a walking eye chart whose monogrammed sportswear hinted she was either Diane von Gucci or Calvin Vuitton. Alas, she was just plain Lilly, a suburbanite, and she was astonished to learn that anyone still lived in the city midst rape and mayhem. Alvin assured her that the security in our hi-rise was so tight that often the residents had trouble getting past the guards. However, we had just signed an agreement to buy a nearby brownstone and Alvin was concerned about our future vulnerability.

"Why don't you buy a dog?" Lilly asked, smiling up at Alvin.

Alvin smiled back. She had just uttered his favorite word. BUY.

Lilly owned one of the few Canaans in Pennsylvania. Protective, friendly, easily trained, Mamaleh sounded like the answer to Alvin's prayers. Lilly showed us photographs of Mamaleh guarding the family manse, Chez Rappaport, a tudor split-level in Gladwyne.

The picture she hadn't meant us to see slipped out of her purse and fell face up on the carpet. It showed Mamaleh rooting through the local garbage cans. In the shadows behind a garage, Lilly's husband Walter, carrying a baseball bat, tracked the spore of the beast.

"Are Canaans smart?" Alvin inquired.

Smart! The Israelis trained them as spies.

"Do they run?" Alvin, the lonely jogger asked.

Not only sprints, but marathons and hurdles!

I tend to be less romantic about purchases, because I usually supervise the repairs. "Do Canaans shit in the house much?" I demanded, to my mind the most significant question of the discussion.

Alvin wouldn't permit his new found friend to answer such a rude question. "Not everything is a joke!" he hissed and waltzed Miss Lillian out to the terrace. They whispered together under the stars. He wrote something down in his little black book—the name and address of the local breeder.

The Hoffmanns in Emmaus, Pennsylvania, handled Alvin's midnight telephone call with aplomb. They were out of pups, even at that hour. The next morning Alvin aroused the only other source of Canaans in the United States, a priest in Tulsa who mated Canaans and Samoyeds in the kennels behind the rectory. It was a rather perverse hobby for a celibate, I thought.

The padre had one puppy left—the runt of the litter, available at bargain basement rates. Alvin wired a deposit and the dog was put on layaway. Our six-year-old son Steven selected the name for our pet. He chose Spot over Rover.

To prepare Spot for his young master, the breeder hired a

young boy to play with the dog every day. I felt it unnecessary to disclose Steven's past relations with livestock. I was sure he had outgrown his former compulsion to swing dumb beasts in the air by their tails. At three, Steven really had had good intentions. He sincerely believed that Jimmy the cat enjoyed his flight training.

When Spot's papers arrived, we found that the breeder had not told all either. Spot was a reservoir of recessive genes. Chief Hatikvah was his only male relative. His mother, Peera of Tel Aviv, posed on the cover of the brochure between the breeder and a hairy white Samoyed. Peera looked like she shed the least.

When it was time for Spot to come east, TWA flew him to Boston in error. Not a good omen. Were the gods hinting that we should control our pride and buy our boy tropical fish? When Alvin and Steven finally brought Spot home from the Philadelphia airport, Alvin had to carry the pup across our threshold because Spot was too zonked to walk. He had been overdosed on valium to help him endure two days in a crate.

Spot looked like a movie star. Leslie Howard minus a chin. His tail was very hairy . . . like a Samoyed's. From the first, I suspected a half-breed had been palmed off on us. Could it be that muffky-fuffky in the kennels was the real reason behind the discount on our cut-rate dog?

Spot collapsed on the floor at Steven's feet. Steven cooed and patted his head. I stroked his side. His fur was soft and pretty. Most of it stayed in my hand.

At bedtime Alvin and Steven dragged the stoned pooch out for his first nocturnal purge. They assured me they would be back in a jiff. They returned an hour later. My disenchanted boy described their route—one stop at each tree between our front door and the Schuylkill River, and extended nasal analysis of every single fire plug in between, both coming and going.

Alvin filled Spot's bowl with food. The bewildered puppy collapsed before the hearth. We retired to our bedroom to read the letter from the breeder that had been attached to Spot's crate.

According to the good father, only martyrdom stood between Spot and beatification. Spot was a healthy, housebroken, hungry beast with a disposition like St. Francis', and an appetite like Pope John's. Spot did eat whatever was put in front of him. That night he chewed two legs off a new birch bench.

"It was old and ugly," Alvin insisted. "I wanted to get a new one anyway." He hooked a leash to the dog's metal collar, and prepared to take his new jogging companion out with him. In honor of their first run together, Alvin had purchased a new black and white sweat suit, so that he and Spot would match.

When they returned Spot looked exhausted, but Alvin was beaming. "This dog runs like a fucking gazelle!" he announced. Alvin was at work when the fucking gazelle leaped through our back screen like a fucking rocket after he glimpsed a cat strolling along our fence.

Attempts to train Spot have resulted in limited success. I'm not sure whose attention span is shorter, the dog's or his master's. Alvin tried a method described in *Good Dog, Bad Dog*. He filled an empty soda can with coins and taped the opening shut. Each time Spot misbehaved, Alvin dropped the can behind him and screamed. This training taught Spot to restrain his really gross habits until after Alvin left for work. I finally threw the noisy can in the trash. The only command Spot ever learned to obey was "Sit!" I don't know if he's really that dumb, or if that's the only English word he understands.

Spot is an effective watchdog. He barks at strangers and most of our friends, and has filled a real lack in our household. He has become the doorbell that Baron Potts-town, our architect, left out of our renovations.

Spot obviously was afflicted by an entire spectrum of learning disabilities, but he never gave me any reason to believe that his health was failing until last year, when a very professional lady veterinarian came to work at the Southern Animal Hospital.

Dressed in a spotless white coat, with her name and degree embroidered on the pocket, she gave Spot a really thorough examination. No one had ever displayed so much interest in him before. His mouth was a plaque mine. His gums needed scraping. But what she heard through her stethoscope really alarmed her. "How long has he had this murmur?" she asked.

"What murmur?" I replied.

I had always assumed that only Spot's brain was defective, but the doctor told me that the valves in his heart had seen better days. Spot was only four years old, but his ticker was 89. His days were numbered. He was living on borrowed time.

I felt surprisingly sad. "How long does he have?" I asked.

"I'll know better when the tests are completed," she replied. Was it my imagination or did she order every procedure on the form? It seemed callous to ask about fees or question the necessity of sending Spot to his maker with gleaming gums. I picked Alvin up at the office and drove him home so we could discuss the best way to break Spot's imminent demise to our son. Steven sometimes bad-mouthed the dog, but I suspected, that like me, deep down he was devoted to our pet.

When we walked into the living room, Steven was engrossed in a comic book. "I don't care if you take my allowance away for a year," he cried, without even looking up. "I am not walking that moron ever again. He dragged me across Race Street yesterday. After a squirrel. That dog is out to kill me!"

Alvin sat down on the couch and sighed. "Listen, Steven," he said. "There's something I think you should know."

Steven looked up, alarmed. Had he pushed us too far? "I really didn't mean it about my allowance, but that dog is in-sane." Steven looked around. "Where is he? Where's Spot?"

Sounding like a Mortuary College valedictorian, Alvin ex-plained the reasons for Spot's absence.

"Will he die?" Steven asked.

"I'm afraid so," I whispered and cuddled my baby against my breast.

Steven pulled away. "Do you think he'll die before January? Erica's German shepherd should have her pups by then and I know she'll give me one if I ask her. German shepherds are really smart. You should see all the tricks Mitzi knows."

The kid was all heart. Would he bring his new puppy to Spot's funeral as his date?

The following afternoon I picked up Spot, his clean teeth and a dismal prognosis. I was told to treat him normally for as long as I could. That advice cost me ninety dollars.

The scope of Spot's work-up convinced me that the vet had earned a doctorate in billing from the Wharton School. Fifty dollars worth of anesthesia for a dying dog! Was that prudent? Spot's prophylaxis hadn't improved his general health. He staggered into my car. He had deteriorated dramatically in just 24 hours.

The next morning when Alvin took him jogging, Spot set a slower pace. The dog was definitely not himself. He only delivered one third of his normal urine output.

Spot spent the next week digging holes around our nonflowering flowering plum. My housekeeper told Steven that Spot was showing us where he wanted to spend eternity. Alvin no longer had the heart to drag him jogging. Spot just lay around and waited for the grim reaper. He picked at his food. He was trying to tell me he wanted something more tasty than Alpo Beef Chunks for his last supper.

I discussed putting Spot out of his misery with a close friend whose regard for our present veterinarian couldn't be lower. "I wouldn't step on an ant on their say-so," Libby insisted. "You'd better get a second opinion."

Libby recommended we consult with Yale Ginsburg, who had more compassion but fewer frills. No oil portraits adorned the walls of his waiting room. No appointments were necessary either. First come, first served, was Yale's *modus operandi*. His waiting room was filled with barking hounds.

Two females in heat had a restorative effect on Spot. Was there an estrus spray we could use for a tonic?

When our turn came I pulled Spot into a small tiled cubicle. A plain metal table stood in the center of the room. In the far corner, leaning against a steel sink, Yale Ginsburg, in stained Bermuda shorts and a stretched tee shirt, regarded his newest patient.

"Does he bite?" he asked suspiciously.

"No, he's a very friendly dog," I replied.

"That's what they all say," he countered unconvinced as Spot bared his teeth and lunged at him.

"He did nip the appliance repair man," I admitted, "but only twice."

Yale came closer. "You lift him up on the table," he instructed. When Spot seemed calm, Yale patted his head. Within seconds he made his first diagnosis.

"Your dog has fleas," he complained, scratching the curly black hair on his own legs. A few of Spot's boon companions had decided to vacation on Yale's calves. Well, doctor and dog could be dipped together.

Yale put his stethoscope into his ears and listened to Spot's heartbeat. "What did you say was wrong with him?" he asked.

I repeated everything I could remember about Spot's poor defective valves.

Yale listened some more. "How much did they charge you for that information?"

"Ninety dollars," I admitted, "but they also cleaned Spot's teeth."

Yale sighed and shifted his stethoscope back down around his neck. He wrote some notes on Spot's record. "They signed Spot's death warrant for 90 bucks and I'm going to pardon him for 10. There's nothing wrong with this dog. Take him home and treat him normally."

Spot recovered from his psychosomatic infarction as instantly as he was stricken. The following morning, he once more reluctantly jogged at his master's side. It's hard to fault Alvin's analysis of the whole affair. The Southern Animal Hospital was stricken with a defective cash flow and we were the cure.

Things have been back to normal ever since. Through blizzards and floods, heat waves and droughts, the dog and his master go forth twice a day. They now each have a companion every evening, a new neighbor and his poodle Jascha, who is even dumber than Spot.

Jascha remained in an air-conditioned bedroom, while vandals stripped his master's first floor of antique stained glass. Spot and Jascha are betrothed, even though they are both males. There will be no pups, but not through any lack of effort.

Do I really hate Spot? Not this morning. He gazes at me like a forlorn lover. He is in-between shedding seasons and has not knocked down my plants all day with his dancing-bear imitations. On other days when I am about to call the ASPCA and turn him in as a stray, into my mind's eye flashes the memory of Spot's finest hour. I'll never forget the look of innocence in his eyes as he urinated on my sister-in-law's baby grand.

Now, how could anyone, even an animal hater like me, ever reject such a wonderfully sensitive beast?

Waiting for Becky

really very comfortable with my body. I couldn't pose without clothes."

"If you want to wear clothes, that's okay too," Becky assured me. "That can be a statement too."

As I walked back to the living room, all the negative programming I had always received about my body was assaulted by the narcissistic impulse to hang in the "altogether" in Becky's forthcoming show at the Graham Gallery in New York City. Why did I consider my body inferior? Unworthy to be displayed? What was a good body? One that worked, I answered my own question. Well, mine worked pretty well. It had tremendous energy and it hardly ever got sick.

I suddenly found myself accepting Phyllis's invitation. "Okay, I'll do it. It may not be gorgeous but it's me!" I arranged to sit for Becky after Labor Day when I returned from Florida. The idea intrigued me.

That night when I got undressed I took a good look at myself in the mirror. Lumpy hips. A girdle of fat where more fortunate women showed a waistline. A bulging belly bisected by a hysterectomy scar. I looked like what I was—a middle-aged lady whose body had nurtured several pregnancies. I looked at myself again and found myself smiling. What the hell! It would be one less exposure to fear.

My husband Alvin lay spread out nude on the bed reading the newspaper. I switched on the overhead lights. Alvin rolled over on his side and draped the sheet over the family jewels. "I've asked you to pull down the blinds before you flip on the big lights," he said in an irritated tone. "Why won't you do it? I don't want the whole street looking in here."

Alvin really believes that our neighbors huddle at their

windows, their eyes glued to heavy-duty binoculars, panting for a glimpse of his dingle.

"I met Becky Young today. She's the photographer who does the color nudes. We saw her show at Marion Locks last year," I replied.

Alvin grunted. "I don't think this Begin-Sadat agreement will hold up," he announced.

"Becky asked me to pose for her."

That caught his attention. "Nude?" he asked.

"Yeah. I said I would do it. Me and Phyllis. After we come back from Miami."

"It's your decision," Alvin remarked, but I could see he was unnerved. He had turned to the financial section of *The New York Times* and was searching for a quotation on his only stock, Commonwealth United, which had plummeted right off the American Exchange two years earlier. It never occurred to me to invite Alvin to pose with me. A man who believes he has a golden cock can't risk being reproduced in Kodachrome. It might print up brass.

Alvin adores his body and takes very good care of it. He jogs, he plays handball, and he dresses it up in expensive clothes. Last month his body betrayed him. It developed a limp. Alvin hired an exercise therapist to set up a program of calisthenics that would stretch his muscles and make him more limber.

Abe came to our house every Monday afternoon at five to work out with Alvin. Alvin taped each session and repeated the workout by himself on the days that Abe was torturing other people elsewhere.

I have always hated exercise, but the following Monday I followed Abe up to my son Steven's third floor bedroom— easily the hottest room in the house. Alvin is convinced that sweating contributes to longevity.

I hopped a few times. I swung my arms around wildly. I did four deep knee bends. I made the big circles reputed to prevent dangling triceps in the upper arms. I giggled and made wisecracks and drove Alvin into a frenzy. He knew he would hear the same jokes every afternoon on the tape. I actually completed three sit-ups before I collapsed in a pool of sweat on the floor.

I worked out with Alvin the rest of the week, cringing at Monday's jokes. The following Monday I spoke less and exercised more. I completed seven sit-ups before swooning. During the trip, I worked my way up to 45 on the West Coast of Florida. By the time we got back from Miami, I looked trimmer but the numbers on the scale were still high. I began to jog in the morning and I went on a diet.

I rarely remain on any diet for more than 30 hours. This time I miraculously persevered. Instead of hunting for Steven's hidden chocolate bars in the fireplace, I chomped on negative calories. I turned my back on an entire round of creamy St. Andre cheese at a party. My will power amazed me until I admitted it was all vanity. I was determined to display a passable body on the wall of the Graham Gallery at Becky's forthcoming show.

Picture day arrived. Steven left for school. I jogged for my usual eleven minutes and was back in the kitchen by five minutes after eight. Alvin is usually dressed by that time and on his way to the office by 8:30 A.M. I carried the milk into the kitchen and discovered Alvin sitting at the table reading the morning newspaper. He was wearing a brand-new royal blue ribbed terrycloth bathrobe.

I scrambled two eggs for him and poured him a cup of coffee. Alvin usually attacks his food as though it is an apparition that will vanish with its steam. That morning he picked at his vittles like one of the Southern belles in *Gone*

With the Wind. Why was this morning different from all other mornings?

I poured myself a cup of black coffee and sat down facing him. No food for me. I simply could not afford to activate any phantom gas which might pump up hitherto hidden bulges.

"Is there any more coffee?" Alvin asked, turning to the Sports page, which he normally never reads.

"I thought you would be at work already," I replied through clenched teeth.

"What's your rush? Why are you in such a hurry to get me out of the house?"

"Becky's coming to take my picture this morning."

"Oh, yeah. Yeah. That's right. I forgot all about that."

"Then how come you're sitting down here all gussied up in your new blue robe? How come you're not wearing that red, blue, and gray rag you usually wear?"

"When I opened up my closet this morning, this robe just fell out into my hands," he explained.

I went upstairs to shower. Alvin followed me. I locked the bathroom door. I needed privacy. I had important decisions to make. Should I shave my legs? They looked a little overgrown but I chose truth until I stepped out of the shower. The wet hair looked very unaesthetic to me. I ran Alvin's razor down the fronts of my legs from my knees to my ankles. It was only a mild compromise.

After I dried myself, I stepped into my robe and attacked my face with unctions and ointments that had been guaranteed to transform my cheeks into a baby's ass when I bought them three years ago at Elizabeth Arden's.

I was on the verge of mild success when I heard Alvin cry out, "Myra! Can you come into the bedroom for a minute, please? I want to show you something." There was real urgency in his voice.

Terrified that one of his moles had turned cancerous overnight, I raced into our bedroom.

"Look at that! Matisse murals painted right on the living room walls!" Alvin waved the Neiman-Marcus catalog of reproductions from Nelson Rockerfeller's collection at me.

Boy he was really nuts today.

"What do you think of this bird?" He pointed to a sleek monolith on the cover.

The question was a dead giveaway. "I think you want to be in my picture, but you're afraid to strip."

"No. Not me. I have to get to the office," he protested, but he did not rise from the oak rocking chair.

I had hit the bird on the brain.

As I walked downstairs, I heard Alvin turn the shower on. A few minutes later Becky arrived. I heated up coffee for her while she set up her camera and tripod and glanced around the kitchen. "I think we'll start over there." She pointed to the kitchen table. I unzipped my robe and sat down naked in the sunlight.

Alvin appeared in the doorway all dressed for work in a brown pin-striped suit, carrying a red and blue tie in his left hand. "Is this tie okay with this suit?" he inquired. Alvin is color blind and sees green and brown as gray.

"No."

"What color is this suit?"

"Brown."

"Oh," he said, slung the tie around his neck and waited to be introduced.

"Alvin is usually at the office by now," I explained to Becky. "He's hanging around because he wants to be in the picture, but he just won't get undressed for us."

Alvin moved backward towards the stairs. "No. No. I'm late. I have important appointments this morning," he protested.

"Would you like to sit down beside Myra just the way you are?" Becky asked.

He pulled a chair over before Becky finished her question. He had been afraid she would never ask.

Alvin really looked dumb with maroon horses draped over his lapels. "Why don't you put on your robe?" I asked. "You'd look less conspicuous in that."

I didn't have to tell him twice. He raced out of the kitchen and returned in seconds carrying his robe in one hand and unbuttoning his shirt with the other. "Will my shoes show?" he asked.

"I don't think so," Becky replied. "The table will hide your feet."

Alvin wrapped the robe around his body and tied the belt snugly. I couldn't help smiling. His hands were folded before him like a sissy schoolboy. A heavy watch guarded his right wrist. Thick eyeglasses masked his stiff face and a bushy moustache concealed his thin upper lip.

Becky snapped away. "Oh, that's wonderful," she pealed. "Just wonderful!" She looked up and smiled at Alvin. "You have a wonderful face," she told him.

Alvin smiled in agreement.

"Such a wonderful tight little face," she added.

When Becky pulled the table out of the foreground, Alvin removed his shoes, socks and trousers. The blond hair on his muscular legs glistened in the sun.

"Now, take off your shorts," I teased.

"I can't. People are waiting for me . . . appointments."

The threat of exposure was making him remember the clock.

I would have understood such reluctance from a man who disliked himself, but Alvin stands in front of the bathroom mirror and strokes his chest for hours.

"I don't stroke myself," he mumbled which indicated to me that his memory was beginning to go even as he was reading my mind. I didn't bother even to discuss it with him. I merely rolled disbelieving eyes toward the heavens.

Alvin put his suit on again and stood behind me like his old stiff self, while I sprawled across two Prague chairs like a voluptuary on display. Alvin left for work only minutes before Phyllis rang the doorbell. She and I posed in the garden for an hour and then it was over. Becky packed up her cameras. She and Phyllis left. I had to put on my clothes again. I was sorry the session had ended so soon. I had really begun to enjoy feeling free.

I didn't ask when the proofs would be ready. I was not in a rush to see my third-rate body in photogravure. Two weeks later when Becky appeared with the contact sheets, I distracted her with conversation. When I finally opened the Manila envelope, I was shocked and delighted. I looked terrific. My body wasn't third-rate! It was only second-rate!

I flashed the contact sheet at Alvin when he came home from work. He reacted to my enthusiasm with considerable restraint. He had spent his formative sexual years in post-World War II in Occupied Japan among skinny, subservient hookers. There is no rational way to defeat conditioning like that.

I hid the contacts in the bottom drawer of my desk, so Steven wouldn't find them. I didn't want reality to upset his Oedipal dreams. But even though I had put the contacts in my desk, I also carried them around in my brain. The thought of 14 x 14 enlargements of me hanging in the Museum of Modern Art made me blush, but I blushed under a big grin.

That evening the Rosans dropped over for a drink. While I arranged snacks on the table, my pictures burned a hole in my head. Helen and Bob are very close friends and real art lovers. It was okay to show them the terrific work Becky did.

The next morning Jeanne Bockenhauer came in to borrow an egg. All she got was the artistic vision of me. When Peter Arfaa appeared to ask Alvin some questions about a sales agreement, he got a surprise treat. In between public displays, I reviewed the images mentally. I could not wait until everyone went to bed so I could be alone with my contacts.

Wallowing in a belated narcissistic fling, I sat down with a magnifying glass trained on the contacts so that I could admire my torso. I had less flab than Phyllis and I looked so much more relaxed than my uptight Prince. His face is a stiff mask. His neck is tense. His clenched toes betray hidden fears. His folded hands protect his manhood.

Of the two of us, he is the more naked.

This Year's
Chic Disease

Anorexia nervosa is a self-inflicted malady which strikes young women who feel they are overweight even when they actually resemble concentration camp internees. Out of a compulsion to appear svelte and chic, they become indifferent to all food and feed instead on the negative fantasies about themselves, along with any marginal supplies of protein still remaining in their muscles.

Salvator Minuchin of the Philadelphia Child Guidance Clinic has developed effective treatment techniques that shun psychic delving. Instead, he involves the family of the anorectic in the cure by training them to react honestly to these games of oral Russian Roulette. He displaces imaginary stress with actual physical encounters which occur when the families of the afflicted, under his prodding, force those girls to eat. I can't decide whether I lust more after the symptoms or the cure.

Before this disease even had a name (when I was four months old), my mother enrolled me in a preventative force-feeding program and triumphed over my indifference to noodle puddings by distracting me with side-splitting tales about a neighbor's son whose nose dripped like a faucet. Whenever I opened my mouth to laugh, another load of carbohydrates slid down my gullet. By the time I was five I weighed as much as many of these Twiggies weigh at 17.

My husband Alvin is waiting for me to turn into an anorectic. He has never seen me eat an entire meal in the 14 years we have been married, and he cannot understand why I still tip the scales at 132 pounds. Around him I truly eat like a bird. At other times, usually while I am waiting for the mailman to drop off that day's rejections, my brain disconnects from my right hand, and I sometimes discover that while I was trying to straighten out a sentence, I ate a quarter pound of butter, just by lifting little dabs to my lips with my fingertips.

Actually anorexia nervosa is my third-string affliction. I prefer metabolic disorders where one has to gorge oneself from dawn to dusk to maintain a weight of 91 pounds. My offers to serve as a guinea pig for thyroid transplants were snubbed by Christiaan Barnard, so I can only look to Brazil now, where crafty surgeons correct God's errors. I understand that real scourges take precedence over my fantasies, but perhaps when saddle bags are wiped out of Southern California, those Rio surgeons will look to the thyroid for a fast buck.

My second choice is a mild but persistent case of dysentery, like the one I nurtured in India last winter, by eating fried foods at the outdoor markets. Being assaulted by lepers is too high a price to pay for being svelte, and U.S. customers will not permit me to import Calcutta tap water.

For the present then, I daydream about being anorectic, teased by reports about teen-age sylphs who consume one entire Cheerio for breakfast or ingest no more than 776⅓ calories a day. I have the same passions, but I cannot triumph over my conditioning. How does one measure one-third of a calorie?

The Anorexia Aid Society in Teaneck, New Jersey accepts contributions to fight this disease. I have sent them my Mom's feeding spoon and a cassette recording of her mealtime myths. Will they honor my request and in return send me an A-N germ? I can dream, can't I? And I do.

I see myself as their poster person, a wraith afloat on a field of sans serif type that cries out:

GIVE!   GIVE!   GIVE!
SEND THIS WOMAN TO LUNCH AT LUTÈCE!

Teen-Age Runaway

Spot is a slender black and white dog who is considered a pure bred Canaan by the Israeli Kennel Club, a mongrel by most veterinarians and a blooming idiot by me. Spot's family tree includes jackals, desert dogs, Peera of Tel Aviv and I suspect, several horny Bedouins. Canaans are supposed to be smart. Many were trained by the Israeli Army to sniff out explosives and carry messages to the front. Spot prefers to make love, not war. Like a pig who can root out a single truffle in an entire forest, Spot can dig up a single chicken bone in Fairmount Park. If some commercial use is ever found for Colonel Sanders' leftovers, Spot will be worth his weight in gold.

My husband Alvin's initial solitary attempts to train our dog all ended in failure. At my urging he finally enrolled Spot in Obedience School at the YWCA when Spot was two. Computed in dog years that made Spot 14 or 15, hardly the most receptive age for acquiring basic skills.

On Monday evenings Alvin and Spot toddled over to the gym at the Y where drooling St. Bernards transformed the already slick floor into a Slideteria. Howling beasts dragged their reluctant masters with them on a nooky hunt. Spot was one of the most crazed. Instead of heeding the instructor's orders to heel, Spot harkened unto the voice of the Lord which commanded him to be fruitful and multiply.

Watching Spot and Alvin do their homework was like watching a circus comedy act rehearse. When Alvin called,

61

"Stay!" Spot jumped. When Alvin cried, "Come!" Spot lay down and panted. Spot only performed when Alvin's commands were followed by an obscenity. I restrained my impulse to turn Spot in as a stray because Alvin and Spot were so *simpatico*. Eric Severeid's doubts about the survival of the human race was their favorite soporific.

Our conflicts about Spot's survival were almost resolved on the eve of his graduation from Obedience School when neighborhood youngsters, celebrating the Fourth of July, set off cherry bombs while Spot was once more marking off his territorial imperatives. Spot leaped over two hedges and galloped toward 20th Street, a major traffic artery.

Alvin ran after him shouting commands. "Stop. Stay. Heel. Sit. Sit! Sit, you dumb son-of-a-bitch!"

Spot thinks that last phrase is his nickname. He sat down in the middle of traffic. Alvin dragged him back to safety, but before Alvin could clip the leash to Spot's collar another cherry bomb exploded and so did Spot. Alvin and Spot left the starting gate together, but Alvin never finished the heat. The dog ran like a jaguar and Alvin lost sight of him at 21st and Chestnut.

Alvin came home despondent and breathless. "Spot ran away," he gasped.

I tried to conceal my glee.

Alvin's grief was tempered with pride. "You should have seen him go. I bet Spot ran 60 meters in two seconds flat!"

Alvin could not endure the anxiety of waiting for some misguided Samaritan to decipher Spot's dog tag and contact us. Within minutes he revealed a preliminary search plan. "We'll get in the car and drive around the neighborhood. I'll call Spot's name and you wave a small steak out of the window." The local strays would have held a mass christening for lesser treats.

Alvin's second scheme was only slightly less irrational. He pushed Jascha, Spot's perverse paramour, into the back seat of our auto and rolled down the window so that Jascha's musk could waft. Jascha is notorious for his inability to control his sphincter around Persian carpets. (His droppings are euphemistically called Mt. Everest by the neighborhood children. Only the Almighty surpasses him in the creation of peaks.)

While I tried to repeat some of the horror stories I remembered about Jascha's behavior in cars, Alvin drove and worried. Suppose Spot got a whiff of his beloved across an Expressway; would he bound into traffic and be killed? I didn't think we would be that lucky. Spot would probably just be crippled for life.

Everytime Jascha barked, Alvin slammed on the brakes and they went out on patrol. Together they charted every fire plug in center city. After Jascha was bone dry, he lay down and whimpered. It sounded to me like he was getting carsick. Alvin raced home and returned Jascha to his master before he created any new mountain ranges on our back seat.

We walked back to our house and sat down on the front steps. No insane barking greeted our approach. "I hope Spot didn't fall into the clutches of cruel people who'll mistreat him," Alvin sighed. I didn't want Spot to suffer either. My prayers that he be blessed with a swift and merciful death were interrupted by the ringing of a telephone.

"Is that our phone?" Alvin asked.

"I think it's the Arfaa's," I lied.

He didn't believe me. He unlocked our front door, grabbed the receiver and heard a gentle voice ask, "Do y'all own a dawg?"

Alvin whooped with joy. The moron had been found.

Spot's savior was unable to remember his house number. His wife, between peals of laughter, managed to repeat an address about four miles away.

When Alvin told her there was a reward for finding Spot, she only laughed harder. Was she a Rothschild or had Spot been rescued by an escapee from Pennhurst?

"Leave your handbag and watch at home," Alvin instructed. His initial relief had been replaced by suspicion. He grabbed his keys and a ten-dollar bill for the reward and off we drove off to 6th and Pine.

Spot had wandered into a mansion. We could see that his savior was a doctor on call by the beeper at his waist. He was also high, but hardly threatening unless one required an accurate diagnosis.

In the family room Spot lay on the couch beside a dozing crone in a stained housedress whose left hand stroked his mane. Spot was too occupied to notice our entrance. Curled up in a half moon he was engrossed in an activity he had perfected in our living room—autofellatio.

Spot's climax awoke the sleeper. "Ah, the top of the mornin' to you on this wonderful afternoon," she mumbled. Then she whispered to one of the children, "Who the hell are they?"

"They own the dog," the kid replied.

"What dog?" she asked.

"Do you live here too?" I inquired. Did the doctor make ends meet by taking in roomers?

"No. I live over there." Her finger pointed toward the back of the room where the bar stood. "I just dropped in to help Tommy celebrate the Fourth. You know, Tommy and I are both healers. Tommy! Why don't you offer these folks a drink?"

Alvin accepted a bourbon and water and sat down in

front of the TV. Spot had stumbled into a household that subscribed to Cable TV. I was entertained by the Healer O'Leary.

"Where do you live?" she inquired.

"Near the Art Museum," I was deliberately vague.

"You mean that sweet dog ran here from so far away! Why, his paws must pain him something fierce."

Spot was jumping for bits of hamburger like a Lippizanner stallion. He didn't appear to be in any distress.

"I have two dogs myself, Princess and Tabitha. I love dogs. I have healing powers over animals, too."

"Are your dogs here?" I asked.

Mrs. O'Leary revealed that Princess and Tabitha now resided in Doggie Heaven, a sinister advertisement for her veterinary skills.

"Let me rub the pain out of Spot's paws," she begged.

Spot showed a flash of brilliance. He backed out of the door.

"Alvin," I called. "We have to go!"

"As soon as this game is over," Alvin promised, pouring himself another drink.

No one stood between the healer and the healee. She tripped on the carpet and ended up in front of Spot on her knees.

Spot looked at me helplessly while Mrs. O'Leary rubbed his front paws against her stained green wrapper and then attacked his flank. The game went into extra innings, and so did she. She trapped me on the couch and told me her family history, all great Lords in County Cork. If half of her stories were true, the name of their ancestral castle must have been Bedlam.

When the ball game was over, Alvin watched a comedy show and then the fireworks began. We all ran out to the back of the house, except for Spot. Thanks to Mrs. O'Leary's treatment, he was barely ambulatory. He was still nervous, but Alvin knelt beside him and covered his ears until the noise stopped.

When Alvin tried to stand up, his back didn't. He had pulled a muscle in his thigh that morning jogging, and his back had stiffened up in empathy.

Mrs. O'Leary walked toward him with her hands extended.

"It's only a pulled muscle," Alvin mumbled. "I'll just soak it in a hot bath and I'll be fine tomorrow."

"I'll fix it," she assured him. "You just show me where it is."

"His right shoulder!" I screamed. "He pulled a muscle in his right shoulder!" With Princess and Tabitha guarding St. Peter and Spot moaning on the living room floor, I decided that if Alvin's thigh required the laying on of hands, the hands would be mine.

The next morning Spot's paws were so sore he could barely stand. I had to carry him out into the yard. The 8,000 yard dash had taken its toll. I had dismissed Spot's psychic healing until I heard Alvin cry out in pain. "Myra! I can't move my arm! My right shoulder feels numb!"

A hot shower helped, but Alvin needed an injection for an inexplicable attack of bursitis. Tennis shoulder, my eye. Alvin doesn't play tennis. I was so glad I had flung myself between the O'Leary hands and Alvin's groin. Spot limped around for two weeks. Who knows how long Alvin might have been out of commission?

Spot recovered eventually and went right back to his old tricks. He jumped through another screen door in May and I have spent the entire summer sweating. It beats being surrounded by vermin.

Steven and Alvin insist that it is futile merely to replace screen after screen. They have decided to make one last attempt to train Spot. Here is Steven's foolproof scientific plan.

He wants to buy an electric cattle fence from Sears, and put it in front of the back screen to teach Spot to keep away. This method will be fast and inexpensive. They plan to return the fence as soon as Spot wises up. They have still not agreed on one vital point. How much current will they use to zap the dog? Alvin opts for a 9-volt battery. Steven insists on house current. Spot will have gone to his reward by the time they settle that argument. In Dog Heaven no screens will stand between him and the neighbor's cat.

The Electronic Fish

Last summer the New Jersey State Turnpike Police awarded my husband Alvin a scholarship to Trenton Prep in the hope that a refresher course in basic driving skills might engrave the legal speed limit on Alvin's right shoe. Alvin quickly mastered the entire curriculum, 55 Good 65 Bad, and spent most of his time there analyzing the state of the art of radar detection electronics with the three-time losers. Alvin heard rumors about an almost perfect fuzz finder, a small black box which perched behind the front windshield, lit up, and screamed whenever its sophisticated circuits encountered radar.

Alvin is a conservative lawyer who never permits his clients to fritter away their assets wantonly. In this way he earns enough dough to indulge all of his own whims. On this occasion he showed remarkable restraint. He waited an entire week before locating one of these gadgets.

The day after his driver's license was restored to him, Alvin invited Steven, our 11-year-old son, and me to dine with him at the Gallery, Philadelphia's new snazzy downtown mall. Steven needed shirts for school and I didn't feel like cooking. We were in the car before Alvin could say, "Charge it."

The ground floor of the Gallery features a daisy chain of fast food joints which specialize in transforming chemical additives into ethnic treats by means of microwave immersion. The eateries were adjacent to the 10th Street entrance, but Alvin parked on 9th Street. Why were we taking the scenic route?

I soon found out. The Radio Shack had opened a store beside the Eastern Wall.

"Hey," Alvin called. "Since we're right here, why don't we stop for a minute to pick up our batteries?" Radio Shack awards free batteries to their cash customers once a month in exchange for bombarding their weak libidos with irresistible stimuli. It is an insidious policy.

During a previous battery pickup, Alvin bought four smoke detectors to protect me from premature purdah. Alvin is better at buying than at installing. The four boxes still sit in a neat pile at the back of our basement and we are still dependent on the primitive fire security system Alvin designed when we bought our house—a cracked baseball bat in the third-floor hallway to smash out the windows and allow us to flee across the rooftops from the flames.

DeWitt, Alvin's salesman, huddled behind his counter trying to decide if Alvin were angry or acquisitive. There were no bags in Alvin's hands. He was not returning anything. DeWitt greeted the East Coast Champion Equipment Buyer with an appropriate embrace. Steven, the Junior Champ, eyed the home computers, wondering if he could convince his Pa to buy him one now in return for future emotional support. "Hey, Dad, did you . . ."

"Not now!" Alvin hissed. He would pay dearly for his impatience.

Alvin followed DeWitt from counter to counter, swaying to his siren song. No, it wasn't expensive. Sure, a child could install it. The police were preparing legislation that very minute to stop the manufacture of the Road Patrol Detector because its effectiveness had cut deeply into the revenues that the State had formerly received from speeding fines.

"Well, what do you think?" Alvin asked, avoiding my gaze. He had already handed his Master Charge to DeWitt.

"If it works so good, how come the guy who told you about it was in driving school with you?" Steven repaid Alvin for his insensitivity.

"He waited too long to buy one," Alvin lied. He looked at me again. "Steven and I can install it together," he mumbled.

I am a sentimental cynic and a sucker for paternal intent. What did it matter if we paid a hundred dollars for fifty-three cents worth of wires, if it brought a father and son closer together and kept our child off drugs? I saw Steven turning his back on the pusher. "No, I will not sniff cocaine. My father, with whom I spent so many happy hours soldering, would never approve." In order to sustain this fantasy I had to blot out of my memory the knowledge that Alvin can barely zipper his pants without nicking one of his joints.

On Saturday morning, Alvin and Steven walked to the car carrying the little black box. Ten minutes later Alvin was alone. He and Steven had disagreed about the placement of the holder, Alvin had lost his temper and Steven had retreated to a friend's house to soothe his nerves. Alvin called to ask me to bring him a Phillips screwdriver. With Steven gone, it was my turn to play Nurse Nelly.

Alvin read the instructions carefully, and then asked me to read them. He wanted a second interpretation. The Korean technical writer who had composed the manual had cut too many classes in English idioms. Together Alvin and I concluded that the electric eye had to face a clear spot in the windshield. No metal was permitted to mar its view.

"What are we going to do about the windshield wipers?" I asked. "We can't just rip them off."

"Just wait a minute. Just wait a minute," Alvin cried. He

is an oldest son and does not handle anxiety well.

We maneuvered the base of his new toy around and finally found an acceptable spot beside the passenger's door. Alvin whipped off the tape that covered the stickum. I pressed down the metal holder. We screwed on the little box. *Voila! Fini!* I don't know how to say slightly askew in French.

I went back in the house while Alvin rushed back to the car, unplugged the unit and hid it in the hall closet. We live in midtown and Alvin was afraid that a thief might notice something unusual on our dashboard and feel compelled to ascertain its resale value.

The next morning we drove to the Berlin Farmer's Market via Interstate 295 at the legal 55 miles per hour. Did Black Mariahs line the highway? Not at all. Alvin forgot to take the infernal machine out of the closet. While I drove Alvin consoled himself with the notion that our excursion to New York City the following weekend would provide a truer test of the detector's capabilities.

The day of the test flight arrived. Alvin screwed the device into its holder, fiddled with the knob and adjusted the power so that the light would not flash on without cause. "You better hook up your seat belt," he advised me. "I think we'll make *very* good time today."

Alvin eased the car out of the parking lot. The traffic light turned green. He whipped around the corner and headed for the Benjamin Franklin Bridge.

Suddenly the little black box whined and the red light on its spine flashed on. It remained lit and vocal until we drove past our local diner, a record holder for the speed with which its chef defrosts frozen pizza.

"There are cops hiding down Appletree Street," Alvin announced smugly.

"Why would they hide there?" I replied. Appletree Street is a narrow cul-de-sac, barely wider than an alley. Cars rush by it with the speed of rush-hour traffic on the Long Island Expressway (affectionately nicknamed "The World's Longest Parking Lot").

A glance down Appletree as we passed showed the street to be fuzz-free.

"Turn the power down a bit," Alvin suggested "Maybe we set it too high."

I turned the knob counterclockwise and Alvin turned the car east on Race Street. As we approached Chinatown the device went insane. It screeched like a wounded seagull and its eye blazed as bright as 15 suns. Was it allergic to MSG? The noise stopped once we crossed 8th Street and were back on American soil.

The ride over the bridge was uneventful. We had relaxed and I was salivating over the mental image of quenelles at Lutèce when Ponzio's Diner appeared in view and the shrill warning issued forth once more. Was this device a radar detector or a restaurant critic?

Alvin had no great desire to commute to Trenton Prep again. He slowed down. We looked around but saw no police. Alvin stopped at the next gas station and we both examined the manual again. Armed with the assurance that we had followed the instructions perfectly we drove back out on the highway.

On the Turnpike, Alvin maneuvered the car into the fastest lane. He didn't stay there long. The screeching started and did not cease until we were well past the RCA facility near Exit 4. Each time we neared a Howard Johnson, our early warning system forced Alvin to shift to a more leisurely lane. It took us two and a half hours to drive to Manhattan. Alvin was not amused.

When DeWitt saw Alvin's terrible face pressing against the glass the following morning, he slipped away for an unscheduled brunch and permitted one of the newer clerks to bear the brunt of Alvin's wrath. The fuzz finder was not defective. It was activated by all forms of radar signals, including microwave oven emissions. In short, it couldn't tell a cook from a cop. *Caveat emptor.*

Today the gadget sits on its dashboard like an electronic Helen Keller. We never turn it on. Instead my eyeballs scan the horizon and whenever I see an unmarked car parked under a bridge or notice an automobile with lettering on its side door hurtling toward us, I sock Alvin meaningfully on his driving leg. We have no statistics that would indicate the rate of recidivism of Alvin's classmates, but he has not received one speeding ticket since my circuits have been deployed. His leg, however, has been taking a hell of a beating.

Goin' Out Among 'Em

The first thing I did after I got married was to take out a new library card. As Myra Daskill I had been on the "Ten Most Wanted" list at our local Atheneum. My second move was to join a few cultural organizations. I was bored with my tried and true friends. I wanted to spread my wings and mingle with a more interesting crowd. In other words, I was ready to social climb.

My fantasies were in technicolor, Paramount Pictures, circa 1940. I saw myself as a Betty Hutton wowing the swells with my style and wit. Discreet whispers would follow my departure. "Who is she? Where has she been all season? We must invite her and that brilliant husband of hers over for cocktails at once!"

My brilliant husband, Alvin Meyer Chanin, Esquire (also a C.P.A.), had graduated in the top of his class at Penn Law School and had been beaten out of the house-counsel position of the Philadelphia Gas Works by a classmate with no academic standing . . . just a few Roman numerals after his Christian name. Alvin tried collection work and criminal law, and then found a niche in torts. He had no social aspirations. I had to appeal to his greed.

"Meeting those people might be very good for your practice," I suggested. "They'll see how clever you are and hire you to handle trusts."

Alvin has always been hard to snow. "The only way I'll

get any work from the Pews is if their chauffeur rams a client of mine in the rear!" Alvin replied.

Baron Pottstown, an obscure architect and former swain, provided me with a more sympathetic ear. Baron was almost as baseborn as Alvin, but he hid his origins under a smoother veneer. Unsuccessful plastic surgery had converted his hooked beak into a Roman nose. It leaned to the right like the Tower of Pisa. Romantic graying locks and a high forehead gave him the appearance of a dethroned Balkan prince. Out of vanity, he refused to wear his spectacles at parties and after gulping down two scotches to calm his anxiety, he stumbled blind and blotto into the very folks he longed to entice.

Alvin was impressed with the dexterity with which Baron wielded his fish knife, but not optimistic about Baron's prospects of finding architectural clients among the Upper Crust at charity balls.

"Find yourself some poor, hairy, short, myopic, ambitious slobs and be nice to their wives till they're rich enough to become clients," Alvin told him.

Alvin is short, myopic and hairy.

Undaunted, Baron suggested we all join the Zoo and the Academy of Natural Sciences. According to him the Gladwyne gentry were into fauna. Just in case they were into flora, too, I sent a check to the Pennsylvania Horticulture Society and I joined the University Museum to mingle with the intellectual swank. I bought a marked-down Geoffrey Beene at the Tribout Shop at Wanamaker's and impatiently waited for the social season to begin. Finally an invitation from the University Museum dropped through my mail slot. For fifteen dollars each, Alvin and I could dine in the Museum's Rotunda and hear some Reports from the Field. It would do for starters.

Baron's date, Yvonne, was a flutist with massive lungs who never wore confining undergarments. She was a sensation in orange jersey. I looked smart but matronly in the Beene black wool. Alvin and Baron wore new double-breasted blazers.

We were incorrectly chic. The Quaker Ritz were into doing good, not doing well. The gents all flaunted color-coded ties which announced their prep school affiliations. Alvin's blue paisley with red paramecium rampant was an indication of more humble origins—above his grandfather's barber shop at 40th and Girard.

Alvin grabbed an aisle seat, and dozed off before the lecture even started. Baron, Yvonne and I listened to "comers" in archeology endlessly extoll their own potsherds. When the lights flashed on, Alvin was refreshed and famished. He dashed up the marble steps past a tall blond receiving line into the South American Indian Room where bottom shelf booze and *cruditées avec dip de l'onion* were available.

Daintily sipping cheap sherry, I leaned against a case of lethal weapons and smiled. No one smiled back. Yvonne was assaulted by toppling ancients, but as for me, the two bluebloods Baron brought over were horrified by my hostile wit and fled back to the bar as quickly as decency permitted. I switched to gin and tonic and strode back to the curare display prepared to avenge these insults to the granddaughter of the adopted son of the grandson of the *Bal Shem Tov*, the wonder-working rabbi who founded the ultra-orthodox Chasidic cult. Yvonne was chatting with a rococco gent who stared at her bosoms as though he were interviewing a wet nurse. "What kind of work do you do?" he asked hopefully.

"I play the flute," she replied.

His eyes bulged with his own prurient fantasy. Hopefully

she would not be listed as the cause of death on his autopsy report.

"Could I hear you play?" His breath came faster and he licked his lips.

Yvonne hesitated. He looked too fragile to survive an audition.

"I'm on the Board of the Orchestra," he wheezed.

"You better ask your wife to toot your flute," I snapped, but this true music lover ignored my rancor. Instead, he reached into his pocket with trembling fingers and extracted his card for Yvonne. As he limped off, Baron scooped her up and we went in to dine.

The food was fresh and tasty . . . what there was of it. The miniscule portions didn't disturb the swells. By dinner time most of them were too drunk to eat anyway. Our table stood at the exact point in the rotunda where the amplified echoes of hysterical laughter merged. The din squelched any attempts at polite chitchat by our tablemates, four bores from the boondocks, who took umbrage at my Polish jokes and left very early.

"Why did I have to spend thirty dollars to talk to you and Baron and Yvonne?" Alvin asked when we got in the car. "I can do that at home for nothing."

"The broccoli was delicious," I countered defensively, which reminded Alvin that he was still hungry. We stopped at a diner on our way home for a little snack.

Undaunted by my first failure I intensified my assault on the local peerage. Alvin napped through lecture and downed countless Air Pakistan surplus meals. Whenever he pointed out that the 400 did not seem anxious to become the 402, I reminded him about Robert Bruce and the spider.

*

A few weeks later Baron telephoned just as I was opening our hand-addressed invitation to the Preview Dinner of the Philadelphia Flower Show. He had already researched the list of patrons in his second-hand Social Register and was beside himself with glee! This was definitely the big one!

Alvin was also beside himself when he noticed the price of admission. "A hundred and fifty dollars for a lousy meal! You must be out of your mind!"

"It's black tie. You can buy a new tuxedo," I replied. Alvin lusts after clothing as much as I long for social acceptance. He polished his studs while I wrote out the check.

Baron's guest this time around was a young woman who wrote a weekly gardening column in the *Daily News*, and introduced me to the botanical elite. They resembled the walking wounded, crones in wheelchairs, gentlemen with broken tibias and canes, who all grew African violets. Did the time these poor souls spent in damp greenhouses adversely affect their bones, or did nips of brandy among the posies instill in them a reckless disregard for misplaced hoes?

The lame and the halt conquered their handicaps in the race to the bar and ditched me and my badinage beside the hors d'oeuvres. I picked at a chunk of Wisconsin Colby and cased the joint for members of the Fourth Estate. A local society editor, her armpits soaked with sweat, waddled by me throwing kisses to others. Perhaps I might score better with the photographer in her wake. He looked too young to know who was who.

He dropped his Nikon when I announced that I searched through the Bulletin for examples of his art, and that to me the shadows on his pictures of smash-ups on the Schuylkill

Expressway offered a new approach to disaster.

He stared at me like I was an escapee from Bedlam. "The shadows are from the flash. They make me use it," he explained earnestly, hardly the response I had hoped for. Had I wasted my time? Was he too innocent to be corrupted?

I assured him *his* use of the flash was really unique.

"Do you really think so?" he smiled and quickly dropped his guard. Until we sat down to dinner I clung to his side like epoxy, except when he clicked his shutter. Then I was always in camera range. How Baron would be impressed when I appeared in the newspapers between Lessing Rosenwald and Clive Driver . . . or peering over Ernesta Ballard's left shoulder . . . or smiling in the foliage behind F. Eugene Dixon and the Wilmington Grange.

There was no mention of the Preview Dinner in the weekend newspapers, but Baron brought an early edition with him on Monday when I met him for lunch. My heart fluttered as he turned to the society page. There they were! His photographs! Even from a distance I could recognize Ms. Ballard and old "Fitz" Dixon. When I leaned closer my pot of gold quickly turned into dross. Caramba! Some son-of-a-bitch in the retouching department had airbrushed out my face.

An even more crushing blow was dealt to me a few weeks later at a disease gala. I was seated with service personnel who had won the meal as a raffle prize. I'm not a person who accepts defeat easily, but even I admitted I was licked. It didn't make sense to throw away money on social climbing that I could put to better use buying caviar. Baron would have to search out architectural clients without me. Alvin was relieved to find those big envelopes unopened in the trash compactor.

In January Alvin came home with a big surprise. *He* was taking me to the Preview Dinner this year. Had he undergone some change of heart and developed social aspirations? Nah! The negligence king, to whom Alvin referred his most maimed clients, had bought up an entire table and invited his most reliable sources of business to join him as his guests.

On my way to our seats by the Western frontier I passed the table of Gwendolyn Berganza. "It was I," she insisted. "I, who singlehanded made spaghetti chic!"

I heard equally pretentious remarks from the ten Boehm bird collectors who shared the next few hours with me and informed me of their latest acquisitions. Lord, what a bunch. Boring. Boring. Ambitious, aggressive, *arrivistes*, reaching toward social acceptance with little hope of gaining it . . . just like me.

The $147 Ratatouille

I have always been a killer of plants. When I enter a room, they cower and shake. They turn yellow. They shrink into themselves. It is as though they immediately understand that I am unable to concentrate for more than five minutes on anything that does not end up in my mouth.

I have a more salubrious effect on dead animals and vegetables. My casseroles blossom. My stove produces gardens of delights. But I, who love to cook and eat more than anything else in life, always dreamed of the day when, like my ancestors in the Ukraine, I would pick fruits and vegetables grown by my own labors, pop them into my pots and make ambrosia. One day my dream came true.

When my husband Alvin, our nine-year-old son, Steven, and I moved into our 100-year-old center city town house, it was bare of green. A flowering plum tree which displayed three small white blossoms each May dominated a small backyard where only trumpet vines, impossible to kill, flourished. Millions of gray squat bugs skittered to and fro across the ancient bricks. But it was a perfect garden for me. Here, in a plot of dirt three feet wide by ten feet long, I would plant my farm.

In keeping with my usual habit of first doing, then asking, I ran out to a nearby seed supply store and charged everything that struck my fancy to my Visa charge card— bales of mulch, bags of topsoil and the most expensive plant food that money could buy. I also came back with strip tapes of lettuce and scallion seeds, a dozen yellow plastic pots, several green troughs, one pepper plant, one musk-melon plant, and one eggplant plant.

My next door neighbor, Peter Arfaa, an Arab with a love of oases, had already furnished me with an excessive supply of tomato plants of the wrong variety, but I could not break his heart. I planted half of them. My husband, Alvin, had Peter cut back some of the unnecessary branches of our non-flowering plum tree so that the sun's rays could fall on my farm-to-be. I sat down in my air-conditioned house to read *The New York Times Book of Vegetable Gardening,* whereupon I discovered that I had done several things in-correctly. I should have dug out, or at least shifted, the shards of old bricks that had been strewn around by previous inhabitants.

I planted the rest of my veggies one by one in the yellow plastic pots in the bottoms of which my son Steven had carefully drilled drainage holes. I sowed the troughs with strips of the lettuce and scallion seed tapes. I placed them in a spot that was bathed in sunshine. I bought a giant hose, watered them all daily (when memory served), and kept our dog, Spot, out of the yard and away from them.

I WAS A FARMER. I now had important matters to discuss with my friends in suburbia. We talked about blights. They were under constant attack. I only had to con-trol my own zeal. They were assaulted by marauding rab-bits. They were overrun by killer weeds. I had a tendency to overfeed, the result of an unfortunate disdain for printed instructions.

My peppers began to form. Both of them. My muskmelon climbed up its trellis, flowering like mad. I suspected the eggplant would give birth to triplets. I even saw the em-bryos of the tomatoes take shape. I was thrilled, enchanted.

Who needed flowers, anyway, with millions starving?

Was it an impossible dream for an urban dweller? My suburban friends fared worse than I. Out in Broomall green hornworms attacked the tomato plants. My friends were too busy to talk on the phone. They were out dusting and spraying. All was quiet on my front, I smugly reported, until the morning that I found the top of one of my tomato plants gone. Several of the leaves on another looked as if they had supplied a midnight snack for another hungry pair of jaws. I searched the yard. The brutes were nowhere to be found.

After three surprise reconnaissance missions yielded no information, I surmised that the pests were nocturnal eaters. So I set my alarm to wake me 15 minutes before dawn. I got up and sneaked down to the yard, camouflaged in a dark green robe, muddy Earth Shoes, and my gardening gloves. No poisons, sprays, or dusts for me.

One of the hornworms yawned in my face when I grabbed him. His companion was more agile and quickly disappeared behind the fence as soon as he sensed my intentions. I examined the one in my hand. He had antlers. His huge jaws were still chomping on my precious green leaves. White rice-shaped eggs clung to his back. He was very ugly.

Intellectually I understood that he was part of the ecological system, just as I was. That did not interfere with my hating him. The sight of the rice-shaped eggs riding on his back snapped my control. He'd brought his whole family with him! I crushed the entire clan under my shoes.

Because my farm was so small, I had small blights but great delights. The lettuce ripened first. We had a small but very tasty green salad. The death of the muskmelon was a blow, but overcome. The rest of the crop grew slowly, despite my overfeeding.

I bought several new books, which gave me several new

tips, which meant several new purchases. The tomatoes got a little bigger and then stopped expanding even though I watered them like mad, which two of the three new books insisted I should do. I threw on more mulch. The tomatoes turned red, but both peppers and the two-and-a-half egg-plants seemed more appropriate for pygmy palates than for ours.

It was the tenth of August by now, and I could no longer delay the harvest. Family and friends were clamoring for a home-grown, home-cooked meal. Finally I set a date. On August 15th I would harvest my crop. I invited several of the poorest cooks I knew to dinner on the following Sunday, August 18th. I knew they would be grateful for a mouthful of anything.

In a crisis I always prefer to tell the truth, so I refused to exaggerate my harvest. I decided to make one teensy but divine casserole out of it.

On the morning of August 15th, I went out and pulled off both dwarf peppers, several slender scallions, all of the runt tomatoes and the two-and-a-half eggplants. They would blend themselves into a *ratatouille*, a French vegetable stew.

Tenderly I peeled, sliced and salted the eggplants. I chopped and sauteed the peppers and the scallions, skinned the tomatoes, fried the sliced eggplants, put them all in a pot on a small flame and simmered them. I cooked it early so that it would have two days to ripen and grow perfect. There wasn't much, but I knew it would be terrific. I tasted a little bit of the sauce when it was almost done. It tasted flat. In the garden I cut some basil and chives and added them. Then I reached into my spice cabinet and threw in a bit more garlic than I had planned to. Well, garlic never hurt anything.

When I tasted it again, the ratatouille was heavy with spices. It also had simmered away to practically nothing, so I could not afford to taste it too often. I decided to let it sit until Alvin came home from the office and Steven returned from day camp. They would make the final judgment. I was obviously too involved to be impartial.

Steven and Alvin smiled as I brought the red casserole over to the kitchen table. I put a scant tablespoon of the stew on small plates in front of them.

"There isn't very much," Alvin commented as he gazed down on his plate.

"I planned to supplement it with a large roast," I replied, defensively offensive.

Alvin lifted a forkful to his mouth and chewed. He looked up at me. "It tastes like garlic-flavored wood chips," he declared.

Steven was far more blunt. "It tastes like shit," he told me as he spit it out. Steven had not quite learned to repress his feelings.

I sat down, pale. I saw before me the Visa bill I had just paid.

"Your family is coming for dinner Sunday," I told Alvin. "They expect a dinner from my garden."

"You better go shopping right now," he suggested. "I'll go with you if you need help."

Together we bought ripe, fresh tomatoes, firm eggplants, baby zucchinis, scallions, and peppers with which to make a proper *ratatouille*. We also bought broccoli and lettuce from my favorite farmers' market. I cooked for two days and was ready to present Alvin's family with vegetable delights fit for a maharajah's table.

While the dazzling roast marinated on Sunday morning, I

ran out into my yard and pulled up every growing thing by the roots, hacked them to bits with an army knife and my kitchen shears, and scattered the remains over the earth. I spread the morning coffee grinds over them. If anyone asked me I would explain to them that I was starting my mulch pit early.

In the end I had opted for the big lie and I did not wish to be contradicted by anyone in my household. I warned Steven that if he told anyone that I had bought all the vegetables I would relieve him of his brand-new skateboard. He knew I meant business and consequently kept his mouth full of broccoli, garlic and breadcrumbs. He could barely speak intelligibly, let alone give my secrets away. I did not have to worry about Alvin's revealing anything; he usually communicated with his family in monosyllables.

Marlene, my sister-in-law, was quite vocal in her praise. "Do you mean to tell me that you grew *these* delicious vegetables in this little backyard?" she asked.

"Not the mushrooms," I assured her. "They were canned."

"Isn't that wonderful?" she sighed.

In September I added up my summer bills and figured out how much the garden had cost to maintain. By applying the principle of cost accounting to my analysis, Alvin arrived at the conclusion that each tomato had cost us $5.17, each lettuce leaf we had swallowed was worth 97 cents, and each pepper had been equal in value to a small diamond chip. Actually his figures were a bit low. I had not included the bills for my garden books.

"Just plant lettuce next year," Alvin urged. "We can have nice fresh salads. Nothing fancy, just lettuce," he pleaded. "Forget about the eggplants and melons and scallions.

They're not right for this climate. They don't grow well here." In one sentence, Alvin had written off the entire agricultural output of the Middle Atlantic States.

As far as I'm concerned, the $147.00 *ratatouille* was a thing of the past. The future lies bright before me. A soil-testing kit is on its way, ordered at midnight from the Sears Farm Catalog, currently my favorite reading. Unbeknownst to Alvin, next season's seeds are tucked away beneath my nightgowns. I am already bored with green things; next fall will bring beets and red cabbage.

I hope the borscht will be more edible than the *ratatouille* was. If it isn't, it can easily be fortified by two quarts of Mother's Pasteurized Beet Borscht. Mr. Myers, in the market around the corner, stocks it regularly.

CB Blues

Our present car, a steel grey BMW, drives as if it were custom designed for Moshe Dayan by Yassir Arafat. When my husband Alvin came home from the car wash without it, I was not surprised, merely curious.

"What's wrong this time?" I asked.

"Nothing," he snapped defensively.

"Then where's the car?"

My cross-examination made him nervous. He ran into the kitchen, removed the duck I planned to reheat for dinner from the refrigerator and devoured all the dark meat before he found an appropriate reply.

"It's not being towed," he assured me. "It's at the CB Villa. I'm supposed to pick it up on Monday." He paused. "I wanted to surprise you."

Surprise me! I was stunned. I followed Alvin upstairs and watched him prepare his skin for its afternoon airing without saying one word. My mind was overwhelmed with the thought of wall-to-wall static. Alvin is 42 percent deaf and finds all sound reassuring. I have ears like a hawk and background noises drive me up a wall. Maybe if I wore ear muffs in the car all the time I might be able to endure the racket.

"Why do we need a CB?" I finally asked.

He was prepared for that question. "For emergencies," he promptly replied.

We live in the center of the fourth largest city in the

United States. What emergency could we possibly have that I couldn't yoo-hoo my way out of?

"Suppose we're driving up to Vermont to go skiing and we run out of gas late at night, or have a flat or an accident . . . " Alvin continued.

"You left out the grizzlies," I replied.

"Look, Myra, I handle lawsuits where unexpected disasters happen all the time, and I just want to be sure that you and Steven are as safe as I can keep you."

I love it when Alvin plays the good father. "You won't play the CB all the time?"

"Of course not," he lied. "It's only for crises. Do you remember last winter when we got stuck in that snowbank near Sugarbush?"

I remembered every terrifying second.

"That's why I got the CB" he assured me as he lay back on the bed and handed me his glasses. "If you're going down would you . . . " he muttered and fell asleep.

I decided to give Alvin the benefit of the doubt. It did make sense to keep a small CB in the car just in case of trouble.

On Monday afternoon Alvin drove the car back from CB Villa. What small CB? Alvin had bought a behemoth. Forty-five channels. An auxiliary generator in the trunk. An electronic microphone, and a power antenna that shimmied up and down on a toggle-bolted switch. Alvin had once again proved himself worthy of the title of East Coast Champion Equipment Buyer.

Steven, the Junior Champ, reacted to Alvin's purchase like a bull does to a red cape. "I need a base station so that I can talk to Dad," he insisted.

"Listen, Steven," I interrupted him. "You don't *need*

a base station. You need water, food, shelter, but you *want* a CB."

"Why did you have to marry an English major?" Steven asked Alvin plaintively. Besides, I was wrong. He needed a CB so he could check out his homework with his friend Josh Broker, a schoolmate who lived five miles away. Josh had sensibly chosen a base station over a puppy dog, Steven revealed. "Why can't we get rid of Spot and buy me a CB with the Alpo money? I have ten dollars of my own that Pop-Pop gave me for my birthday. If you're that chintzy, I'll pay for it myself!"

I pulled Alvin into the kitchen and muttered through clenched jaws, "How do you expect that child to learn to save for things when you have no restraint?"

In the living room Steven was singing a sweeter song. "Come on, Dad. We can just go look. You don't have to buy me anything. I just want to see what they have."

"I really don't spend much time alone with him," Alvin whispered. "I'll just drive him over to the Radio Shack. He has a right to do what he wants with his birthday presents. If I have to add a dollar or two, I'll take it out of his allowance."

Steven's income was fifty cents a week. His financial obligations already approached the national debt. Still the thought of father and son sharing an afternoon turned me into putty. I waved as they drove off toward instant gratification.

Alvin and Steven returned with their idea of a purchasing compromise. One base station for Steven's room, one three-channel walkie-talkie, and a CB version of Fowler's *Book of English Usage*. The purchases showed considerable restraint. Sometimes they come home with two of everything.

Before any of the boxes could be opened, we each had to select a handle. In CBese, handle is another word for a nickname.

Steven chose Iceman for himself because he thinks he's cool. I insisted that Iceboy was really more his speed. I was named Cookie in honor of my culinary expertise. Renaming Alvin presented the biggest problem. Most of my choices would be bleeped right off the air.

"What about T.P.?" I finally asked.

"What's that mean?" Steven wondered.

I didn't answer. Them what needed to know already knew. T.P. stood for Tyrone Prick, a name I had bestowed on my beloved during those portions of our courtship when he was not sure I was worthy of him. He still had not entirely outgrown it.

We settled on plain Tyrone. He and Iceboy lugged the parcels up to the electronic nursery. A half hour later the older boy zoomed out to his car and drove off into the night. When he returned with the walkie-talkie still sprouting static, he was beaming. "You said it wouldn't work. Well, you were wrong. I could hear Steven as clear as a bell. We have no trouble communicating when I'm driving around and he's in his room."

"Terrific," I replied. "Now try answering him when he talks to you during dinner."

For the rest of that month we drove around in a static cloud. Steven replaced me in the front seat so he could man the controls. Up went the antenna as Tyrone and Iceboy searched for life in the void. No one replied to their signals in English. Our CB spoke in "tongues." Steven sounded like a sharecropper to me . . . but not to them. Somehow they knew he was circumsized. Fortunately Steven has a limited attention span. In a few weeks, he was back to disco, and tambourines once again assaulted my eardrums.

Early in October Alvin's nightmare came true. Our car died on Route 70, an isolated road between Pole Tavern and Bi-Valve in southern New Jersey. Alvin didn't even lift up the hood to see what was wrong. Engine design was gibberish to him. Steven and Alvin switched on the CB. The noise encouraged our dog Spot to howl.

"Emergency channel," ordered *père*.

"Gottcha," replied *fils*. He clicked a button until a red 9 appeared in the window of the microphone. He handed the mike to his Dad. This was not child's play. This was *Star Trek*.

"Breaker nine. Breaker nine," Alvin chanted. He stopped and looked up at his next in command. "How do I tell them our motor conked out?"

Obviously S.O.S., understood on every corner of the globe, would not suffice for the knights of the road.

The CB Bible was God only knows where, mixed up with the comic books strewn on the floor of Steven's room. Steven finally came up with an inspired answer. "Tell them our seven-inch ganglerwrench fucked up," he suggested.

Alvin told them, but no one cared. A seven incher was insignificant in CB Land. "Why won't those bastards answer me?" he cried.

"Yewer tawkin' funneh," Steven explained. "Bettah leht me trah."

Steven trahed and trahed and trahed with no different results. They switched from channel to channel. One was in the clutches of the Biloxi Gourmet Society. They were sharing recipes for grits crêpes and catfish quiche. The new food revolution had even reached the hinterlands.

There was a barn about a mile up the road. I decided to walk to it to look for a telephone. I really didn't want to be around when Alvin's disenchantment reached full force. He would find some way to lay the blame on me. I had only tramped about 20 yards when a police car rounded the bend. The officers stopped to ask me what was the matter.

There was a CB in their car. I asked them if they had heard our calls for aid. They hadn't. They only used it to contact the station house. Listening to lawbreakers reveal the exact placement of their radar units really depressed them. But they did call their headquarters and arrange for a local tow truck to come to our aid.

The hick mechanic found the source of the trouble in minutes. Our stall had been caused by our own CB. During installation some wires leading to the motor had been stripped. Those same wires had just shorted out.

A few deft moves with his rusty pocket knife and our buggy was operational again. Our auto had never recovered its health with so few complications. (Our dealer usually prescribes a week of bed rest and plasma shipments from the Vaterland with bills to match.) Alvin questioned our savior about his credentials. He had none. He was just sympatico with automobiles. Alvin carefully wrote down the exact directions to this mechanic's garage. It might pay us to drive to Pole Tavern for inspections.

It was dark now, and we drove in silence, but both Alvin and Steven abhor a vacuum. Without distractions they might be forced to think. Iceboy decided to make one last try at contact on the Citizen's Band. Perhaps the folks in Jersey had lower standards.

"Breakah Wun Nahn. Breakah Wun Nahn," he declared in his best imitation Charlestonese. "Dew yew reed me? Gieve me a copeh."

Suddenly a voice broke through the static. It was Birmingham Billeh. He read us. Ovah.

Hold a conversation with an absolute stranger! Hardly a Chanin trait. Steven is the Crown Prince of a dynasty whose family crest contains a pair of sealed lips. Benny, his grandfather, can't even tell the reservation people at Delta Airlines that we are staying with him. Alvin answers most queries with grunts.

Birmingham Billeh transmitted in vain. It was Steven's turn to get even. Steven really knows how to bear a grudge. Let a Southerner see how it feels to be the voice crying out in the wilderness.

The following week robbers broke into our car. They stole the entire communications console and dented the right metal panel that held those electronic guts in place. We can't replace anything until new parts arrive from the Vaterland. Based on our previous experiences with replacement parts I would project that the repairs to the car will be completed around the turn of the century.

The BMW factory is in the clutches of a Teutonic computer; order rightly takes precedence over mere human needs. I don't want to be quoted, but I think that Martin Bormann is the vice-president in charge of international shipments. If he suspects that the customer is non-Aryan, your order is automatically sent to Bergen-Belsen.

Alvin really misses his noise machine. Rock 'n Roll has rescued him from many in-depth discussions with me about defects in his character. I know that he will find another noisemaker shortly. It's just a matter of time until he's once more seduced by the state of the art.

Yesterday Alvin vanished into the bathroom with the latest Radio Shack catalog. Who knows what overpriced hunk of transisterized shit has caught his fancy this time?

I threw the brochure into the trash as quickly as I could. Was I too late? Only time will tell.

In the meantime Alvin has been comforted by reports that Telestar has sighted our panel in the middle of the Atlantic Ocean. The messenger from Munich has almost reached the Gulf Stream and has switched from the breast stroke to the crawl. Let's hope that Ludwig hasn't made the long swim in vain, and that the right panel (not the left one) is clutched firmly between his incisors this time.

Miami Beach Kink

I have entertained lewd fantasies about Florida ever since I was 15. In reply to a prim request for rates, the Chamber of Commerce flooded me with brochures that showed lovers clinging to each other under tropical moons. The woman wore orchids at her wrist. Her sweat glands were under control and no incipient moustache threatened her social life. Her lover had broad shoulders and an adorable ass. Only his back was ever seen. To me that meant he had such a huge erection that it would have been indecent to photograph him from any other angle.

Carnal desires for tropical nights of bliss still tantalize me. Even today, palm trees, Gulf waters, even the sign that announces the Jacksonville City Limits, inflame my libido. Despite my lustful longings, our trips to Miami resemble fortnightly retreats. My husband Alvin, our son Steven and I go south every August to stay with my father-in-law, Benny, a dancing widower who lives in a one-bedroom condominium with all of Alvin's discarded suits. Our bed and the convertible couch that Benny and Steven share rest against the same thin partition. Since my husband Alvin is reluctant to perform for his next of kin, he plays handball in Flamingo Park with aggressive septuagenarians and I shop in Neiman-Marcus for an effective pimple cream.

Last year we were driving back to Benny's apartment after taking Steven to see *Benji* for the third time. Alvin misread a sign and we found ourselves in an unfamiliar part of Miami. All around us were motels that all began with the same letter—X. Flashing neon signs offered satin sheets, waterbeds, closed circuit porn, individually or in tandem. Mentally I began to clear my appointment calendar so that Alvin and I could spend a night sight-seeing.

When we got home, Steven announced that he wanted to see *Benji* again the following night, but I had more exotic filmfare in mind for me. What was the purpose of a child visiting his grandfather if they couldn't enjoy a movie together once in a while?

"Pop-Pop will take you."

"Why can't you?"

"Alvin has to meet some people on business."

"Who do I have to meet tomorrow night? Alvin asked when Steven went to the bathroom.

"Linda Lovelace and Johnny 'Wadd' Holmes," I replied.

Alvin looked disappointed. Marilyn Chambers is his favorite movie star.

"I want to spend the evening at one of those motels we passed earlier."

"I don't know about the waterbeds . . ." Alvin sometimes suffers from motion sickness.

"Take a Dramamine," I snapped and looked up at him. He looked terrific in his suntan and white shirt. Maybe Steven would fall asleep early.

Steven looked exhausted when he came back into the room, but he was only nauseous. He threw up twice and insisted we leave our bedroom door open in case he needed nursing in the wee small hours.

When Benny came home from the dance at the Legion Club, I called him into the bedroom, too. "I want you to do me a favor."

"All you have to do is ask," he assured me.

"Alvin and I have to go somewhere tomorrow night. I told Steven you would take him to see *Benji*."

"The movie about the dogs?" Benny cringed.

I nodded.

"Listen, I don't mind taking him somewhere. Do you think he would like to go to the Casablanca? They have a nice little disco there for the kids."

Steven was only nine. He still preferred dogs with four legs. "He said he wants to go to the movies," I repeated.

"All right," Benny sighed. "I told Renate that I would take her to the Casablanca tomorrow night. The dance there starts at seven. I'll go there with her for an hour and then I'll come back and take Steven to the movies. Is that all right?"

It sounded marvelous to me.

I stroked Alvin's calf with my big toe while Benny involved him in an analysis of Renate's Real Estate holdings. I dozed off while they were discussing leverage and the kiss that awakened me was Steven's. He wanted breakfast. I whistled while I scrambled the eggs. *Toujour l'amour.* Tonight for sure!

During the afternoon I cruised the Bal Harbour branch of Frederick's of Hollywood for flimsy black lace. After my shower I annointed my erogenous zones with musk. Benny had assured me he would be home before 8:30 but at 9:27 he had still not appeared. At 9:45 my dreams of champagne and caviar disintegrated. Alvin opened the refrigerator door and stripped the shelves as bare as a swarm of locusts would have. He left me half a jar of Gulden's mustard.

"Where's Pop-Pop?" Steven asked looking up from *The Muppets*. "When are we going to the movies?"

"He'll take you to the late show," Alvin promised. "You can take a nap on the way home if you get sleepy."

At 10:15 Benny finally appeared. Renate followed him into the apartment. She carried a small trophy.

"I'm so sorry," he apologized. "It just slipped my mind about the time. You know when you get old. There was a hustle contest tonight and Renate wanted . . ." He blushed.

"My Benny is the best hustler in South Beach," Renate proclaimed.

He certainly was. It was too late for *Benji*.

Steven began to cry.

I fought the temptation to tell Renate that Benny was more turned on by the interest she received from her investments than he was by her dancing feet, but I had no time to spend on nonsense. Time was a 'wastin'. We had to hurry to the motels before a convention of Shriners from Terre Haute commandeered all the waterbeds for an orgy.

We drove for hours. The Strip hadn't seemed so remote the night before. Was the motel like Brigadoon, making one appearance every century? Just as I was deciding that my monastic routine had made me hallucinate, I saw a series of vulgar neon signs. Alvin drove up to the office of the XXXX while I huddled in the car and felt delightfully unwed.

"Did we get the last room?" I asked when he handed me the key.

"Nah. They had plenty of empties."

When I walked into our love nest, I understood why. The Honeymoon Suite looked like a green stucco basement. Pregnant dinosaurs decorated the black chintz portieres. A gray folding door cordoned off the toilet facilities. The decorator had studied interior design at Buchenwald.

I fell back on the waterbed. Yuck! Muslin sheets. I didn't even use muslin for cleaning rags. The floor was covered with stained indoor-outdoor carpeting. There went my dreams of screwing on bearskin.

I bobbed up and down while Alvin fiddled with the TV. At last the horizontal hold triumphed. The same problems we had with our set at home had followed us 1300 miles to Xanadu. Double images. Ghosts. Blizzards. I couldn't tell if I was watching auto-fellatio or an orgy.

A new feature began. Classic porn. The film, about sex in Junior High, had been produced long before the automatic promotion policies had gone into effect. The freshmen looked like they were in their early forties.

The names of the cast flashed on the screen. Behind the type a teacher and a student groped each other. Alvin was close enough to see what they were doing and it had turned him on. Before I could switch into black fringe he grabbed me. To make a short story shorter, Alvin came during the credits and then dozed right off afterward. He had taken a Dramamine earlier to counteract any possibility of motion sickness.

At two in the morning I roused him out of a drugged sleep. I helped him into his clothing and then into the car. He slept like a baby while I drove home. In the parking lot of Benny's building, he revived slightly. "I'm sorry . . ." he mumbled. "Tomorrow."

We embraced while the elevator carried us up to the fifth floor.

"Shhh . . ." he whispered. "Let's try not to wake them." He slipped the key into the lock as deftly as a burglar and turned the knob without a click.

"Hello! Hello! Hello!" Benny greeted us. "Did you have a nice time?"

"Alvin had a better time than I did," I replied.

"Where did you go?" Benny asked in a sing-song voice.

"To Club Sordido."

"What's that? A Cuban nightclub?"

Alvin moved an armchair in front of the TV. "Do you mind if I watch this for a few minutes?" he asked. "I'm still groggy. Would you make me a cup of coffee please?"

I walked over to the sofa-bed to cover Steven and my heart dropped down to my feet. The bed was empty.

"Where's Steven?" I asked.

"Oh, Steven. He is some kid!" bragged his proud Pop-Pop. "Even Renate said he is something, and she don't have too many good words for anybody's grandchildren but her own."

"Where's Steven?" I repeated, dreading the answer.

"He told me that he thinks he has the virus and he wanted to sleep with you in your bed in case he needs to throw up in the middle of the night."

No sense in making coffee and tossing and turning. I made a pot of tea instead. I sipped the hot brew and glanced through a volume of Thomas Merton's poetry to prepare myself for another night in my tropical nunnery, while Benny gave Alvin an up-to-date report on Renate's business affairs. Her partner was robbing her blind. Benny felt very bad that it had taken him so long to ask her to dance.

Greed Conquers Fear At the Bellevue-Stratford Hotel

Only in Philadelphia could a liquidation sale become a media event. All the cowards who had shunned the Bellevue-Stratford Hotel during its death throes from Legionnaire's Disease, fearlessly queued up to salvage cheap nostalgia from its estate. Fortified by greed and soothed by reports of substantial discounts on tomorrow's antiques, they were now ready to risk their health for gain.

Monogrammed mounds of kitchen and bedroom supplies filled the windows of the hotel's deserted shops. "Would you feel funny eating dinner off a plate with a big B.S. on it?" I asked my husband Alvin, the fourth person in line.

"Only if you served lung or spleen," he replied.

At 8:30 the TV cameras lurched around the corner.

A teenager berated her mother while the cameras panned down the line. "If you weren't so dammed cheap we'd own four TV's and I could watch myself on every channel!" I understood her concern. I hoped that the lenses had not been focused on me while I was biting my nails.

The first person in line, an irate "bag lady" begged a reporter to chase the poachers out of her doorway. My psychic attempts to contact the same newsman failed because Alvin kept jamming my transmitter.

"We have to make a list," he insisted. Translated from the Japanese—the vernacular of the Jewish American Prince—that meant he wanted me to take dictation. "If we don't write down what we want now, somebody else will grab all the good stuff."

I could see from that *non sequitur* that Alvin was having an attack of Supermarket Syndrome, a compulsion to acquire worthless objects usually triggered by prolonged exposure to insect sprays. Even though I carried six empty shopping bags and lusted in my heart after copper cisterns, my primary reason for attending the sale was to get media exposure.

The doors finally opened. Alvin and I ran into the lobby. Milly, the elevator operator at the Bellevue since '04, was more interested in giving interviews than she was in manning the winches. Rather than wait until Milly was through with her memoirs, Alvin and I zipped up two flights of stairs to the Crystal Ballroom where rumpled linens and nicked silverplate were stacked on tables that had formerly held 12 Biddles. I arranged service for 12 in a shopping bag while Alvin scoured the room for copper pots. He returned with two real finds—a scratched Art Deco tray and a dented champagne bucket. He also brought me four egg cups even though he knows that even the thought of soft-boiled eggs makes me nauseous.

Our screams attracted several reporters. We divided them. Alvin got Mary Walton of the *Inquirer* and I grabbed the mike that hung around the neck of the radio reporter. He was charmed by my ideas but shocked by my profanity. I would have to be bleeped. After I gave him back his equipment he chatted with a gray-haired woman who had spent her honeymoon at the Bellevue and was buying a used towel for a souvenir. In reply to one of his questions, she revealed how she felt about all those sons-of-bitches who deserted this fine hotel when it needed their fuckin' business and now those same cocksuckers were grabbin' up shit that would be worth a bloody fortune in ten years.

There was no sense in my rushing home. Alvin and I went out to lunch to give the technical crew time to splice out all those words that are forbidden on the air because hearing other people say them offends a majority of middle America.

The first interviews from the Bellevue were played at 7:40 that evening, when Milly revealed everything about nothing. She was followed by the Captain of Security at 8:40 who found the crowds large but orderly and at 9:40 an octogenarian barber described shaving Caruso's golden throat in the Bellevue basement in 1917. Everybody made it but me!

At 11 that evening Alvin appeared on two news program leads without me beside him. The camera had photographed me biting my nails. I did a little better with the newspapers. Mary Walton wrote up our egg cup disagreement in depth. In such a short article, why did she feel compelled to include my age?

I went to bed depressed.

The next morning I was really annoyed when the phone rang at 10 of 8. "Who is it?" I snapped.

"I was sitting on the toilet and I heard your name on the radio," an old friend told me. "You were hilarious."

I jumped out of bed. "How long did I talk?"

"A long time. Maybe five minutes."

I flipped on the radio beside my bed. At 8:40 Milly was back and at 9:40 it was the security chief's turn. I was due at my dentist's office at 10:15 for a complicated extraction. I had a molar that was hanging by a hair, but that hair was attached to a crown of caps. The last cap had to be separated from the others by sawing through the connection.

The remaining caps had to be polished so they would not cut my mouth. Then I had an appointment with an exodontist who would pull the faulty molar. I couldn't cancel such an intricate schedule to sit home beside my radio, waiting to hear my golden voice. I dropped a fresh tape into Steven's portable radio-tape recorder and took it along to Toothville.

When I strolled into the dentist's office carrying a huge AM-FM radio with a tape recorder unit, I felt like the world's oldest living teenager. My dentist did a double take. He was accustomed to seeing adolescents who could not be without noise, but he had never before encountered a Jewish intellectual who could not bear to be without the news. I kept the radio volume high in case my comments were broadcast while he was sawing through my crowns. I didn't even ask for general anesthesia. The anticipation of being a star had raised my pain threshold.

When the time came for me to move on to the exodontist's office, I carried my radio with me, and put it on the floor beside my purse.

Dr. Gillman had been warned that I was phobic about dental pain. He had the injection of sodium pentothal in his hand and a smile on his face.

"No," I said. "I don't want that. Just give me a local and don't make it too strong. I don't want my ears frozen."

I clutched the arms of the chair while he injected the liquid into my gums. After the xylocaine took effect, Dr. Gillman walked toward me holding the pliers.

"Stop!" I screamed and jumped out of the dental chair.

"You're really overreacting, Mrs. Chanin," Dr. Gillman shouted. "That tooth is so loose I could remove it without any instruments."

"Oh, shut up," I hissed and grabbed my radio. "I'm gonna be on the air!"

I pushed the record button and smiled blissfully while I listened to my immortal words. Five minutes, my eye! I wasn't on for more than 50 seconds.

Afterward I sat quietly and let the dentist pull my tooth. I showed him how brave a star can be.

The Frog Princess

I am a Frog Princess. My foot will never fit the glass slipper. My mother, Queen Sylvia, has gnashed her teeth for years, watching less gifted maidens zoom past me during the Motherhood Olympics. Gaining reflected glory from one's offspring is a form of internecine warfare in which siblings duel with each other using the achievement of their children as artillery. The only shell in Sylvia's arsenal was my toilet training, completed when I was 10 months old. After that it was all downhill. My subsequent feats condemned Sylvia to a lifetime of mendacity lest her sisters discover how perverse I really was. I am the Lucy van Pelt to her Charlie Brown. I still yank away the football each time she gets ready to kick it.

She never understood what went wrong. She always imitated her mother's behavior. Waited on me hand and foot. Carried me around like a Torah scroll. Once I realized what she wanted, complete control over every facet of my life, I withheld as much as I could from her and forced her to chase me with every weapon in her arsenal. I always outran the enema bag, but what Sylvia could not conquer by force, she usually won by guile. She laced my pudding with Ex-Lax.

By the time I was four I looked like Humpty Dumpty, but Sylvia complained bitterly that I didn't eat. I turned up my nose at the foods she cooked best, and would not permit her to sneak even pulverized versions past my oral sonar. My taste buds became as keen as the rump of the princess who felt the pea under seventy mattresses. The hopeful look in Sylvia's eyes was a dead giveaway each time she put spinach in my stew. My fat only counted if I got it from her cooking. Hershey bars and hamroll at Dolchanczyk's subtracted points from her score.

My father's sisters knew Sylvia considered them baseborn. They repaid her pretentions through my defects. "Sylvia," Gitel would cry after I refused her greasy dumplings, "What's wrong with Myra. She doesn't eat anything."

Della attacked her flank for the kill. "You better take her to a specialist right away. Don't save money when it's a case of life and death."

I fingered my emergency rations of Halvah while my mother wrestled with the dilemma that would haunt her for the rest of her life. How could she brag about a gifted daughter who was determined to fill her mother's life with shame? Between us always loomed another spectre. Was I a changeling? Had the nurses at the immaculate Jewish Hospital fucked up? Could my genes have been impaired during delivery. Every one of my accomplishments was slightly askew.

I spoke Yiddish perfectly, but I could not learn to read. When I played the lead in the production of *Mottel, the Cantor's Son*, I memorized every word in the script except my own lines. Despite high Stanford-Binet scores, I got insignificant grades. I was concerned about lynchings in the South and extolled the virtues of Stalin.

My mother was a slave to her superego. I stole perfume at the 5 & 10, and cursed like a teamster at home. Instead of revelling over Jewish High Kitsch (Jan Peerce and the "Bluebird of Happiness"), I bought the scat songs of Nellie

Lutcher. I read no classics, just *True Confessions*, and played "Doctor" with the intellectual rear guard.

Sylvia prayed that I would come to my senses at 14, join the B'nai B'rith Girls and prepare for a life of subservient frigidity. My cousin Harriet had started training for a career as a consumer by shopping only at Bonwit's. I was disinterested in wearing apparel. Nothing fit me anyway. Harriet attended parties in order to meet a pre-med. I went dancing at St. Al's low class church with Charlotte Cachione and Dot Dolchanczyk. There I prepped and writhed with future dropouts in the shadow of the cross. Even they didn't find my charms worth a ten minute ride on the subway.

When I was 16 Sylvia introduced me to a neighborhood quack who introduced me to spansules. Wow! How I loved that energy! When one pill stopped suppressing my appetite, I doubled my dose until I was a speed freak ten years before it was chic.

During the day I maintained my bravado, but at night I shared my mother's dreams. I didn't want to be poor, lonely or creative. I longed to stand under the wedding canopy with a specialist, too. Harriet married a medical android with a golden stethoscope. Her future was secure. The demands on her life were consistent. She had to go to the beauty shop, win cleaning competitions with the maid, and take her mother shopping for corsets.

The pre-meds were all snared by others. Bums and car thieves beat a path to my door. My career was even less distinguished than my social life. I dropped out of college and forged trucker's signatures on phony bills of lading so that my employer, a manufacturer who flirted with bankruptcy, could wrest advances from his factors.

Finally someone who really seemed to like me came into

my life. Of course that meant that he was shit. He was clever enough to realize I thrived on rejection, and won my heart by playing it cool. Even my mother liked him at first. Lou was handsome, polite and Jewish.

Lou was an underachieving Pisces who earned just enough money to stage extravagant courtships. He could not agree to marry me because he expected to die at 40, like his father had. My mother watched Lou wear out a seat on her couch without putting a ring on my finger. She began to pray he would die at 28. She was convinced I'd retained my virtue, because Lou and I never stayed out late. He introduced me to matinees, while Sylvia was packing soup mix at my father's store.

Time passed. Harriet's sons were Bar Mitzvahed. Lou and I drank, danced and gobbled up hors d'oeuvres. Sylvia dreaded each new party. She would be assaulted by her peers. "Nu? Nu? Nu?" they asked in a code that she understood only too well. That phrase was an indictment of Sylvia's maternal deficiencies. Her daughter had refused to bend. What dreadful things had Sylvia done that required such awful retribution? My mother didn't understand why she had been cursed, and her fears for the future were correct. Even more shame awaited her.

When I was thirty I finally fell in love with a doctor. He was my analyst and I paid 50 dollars for every hour I spent with him. That was the biggest bargain of my life. He helped me to get an appropriate job and move into my own apartment. Sylvia's hysteria rose to golden heights. God only knew what depraved acts I would commit in my dirty efficiency. Actually they were exactly the same as the ones I performed on her spotless floors. As I began to like myself more, I performed them less and less. Moving out was really bringing me closer to her desires.

She tried to keep my apartment a secret, but word soon got around. Sylvia attempted a Jewish version of hari-kari. Death by palpitations.

I got a better job and moved into a more expensive neighborhood. I began to date more interesting men. Finally Alvin appeared at a dance. Financially stable. Divorced but childless. A lawyer and a C.P.A.

Sylvia's idea of a lawyer was a clone of Paul Muni in *Counselor-at-Law*, a well-dressed, refined intellectual who spent his life in pursuit of justice. Alvin jogged in torn sweat suits and fantasized about managing rock stars. Whenever he met me at Sylvia's for dinner he was chauffeured there by some spaced-out hippie in a psychedelic van.

Alvin screamed "Shit!" and "Son-of-a-bitch!" as often as Sylvia cried, *"Oy, vey is meer!"* My mother could have excused a son-in-law's violent temper, but Alvin was not rushing down the aisle with me. One morning when Sylvia called my apartment at 2 A.M., no one answered the phone. She located me at Alvin's and screamed the wisdom of the ages at me.

"Why should he buy a cow . . ."

I bought my ice cream at Baskin Robbins because they always let me taste.

Finally Alvin gave me a diamond ring I never wear, and his sister threw me a surprise bridal shower. Sylvia gave up the battle against vice and interviewed caterers instead. I got married in a synogogue in a white gown. Sylvia trudged around the hall in pink satin and sequins making sure that everyone there understood that everything was perfect.

Did Alvin's kiss break the spell? Did I become a proper princess like my cousin Harriet, who, despite debilitating attacks of ulcerative colitis, finds time to scrub her kitchen floors and take my Aunt Della to buy brassieres?

I'm still a frog. I still wear blue jeans instead of mink. I wear no makeup at all. My 12-year-old son plays with black children. He doesn't know they're supposed to be bad. I live in the city in an Irish neighborhood. Harriet fights drugs in the suburbs. My house was renovated by a first class architect, but I still drop my clothes on the floor. I often eat lunch with a former suitor, a practice my mother frowns on.

My money gives Sylvia no ammunition. I use it to do as I please. The things in which I rejoice have no meaning for her generation. Alvin and I amuse each other even after 15 years. I have close, loving friends. Two years ago I finally started writing. Unfortunately my stories involve telling the truth about myself . . . and her.

Now publishers write me mash notes. I fantasize about talk shows, best sellers and autograph parties. On the dust jacket of my first book, I wanted a photograph of myself in which I perch naked in my kitchen. I'm no playmate but I was convinced that picture would sell my book. But my publisher was just as convinced that the world was not ready for a middle-aged centerfold. I will have to make do with being the invitation for Becky Young's Philadelphia show.

Success! But at what a price! The final twist of fate's knife in my mother's heart. How will she claim the credit for such perverse fame? Her unnatural daughter, the Frog Princess, displayed in her birthday suit in art galleries all over America.

My physical exposure can be blamed on corrupt retouchers, but what excuse can my mother give for the messy countertop beside my left tit. Five minutes after my Aunt Della turns her jaded eye on the disarray behind me, everyone Sylvia cares about will know that her daughter is still a lousy housekeeper.

Swathed in Blackglama

As a result of an automobile accident which gave me a slight whiplash and a medium-sized depression, I acquired a small nest egg, courtesy of the State Farm Insurance Company. I plan to use my savings to comfort me in my old age. I want to die of a beluga caviar overdose at the Cheap Home. Only the most pressing emergency would force me to dip into my reserves. On May 5, 1979, one occurred. It was my 46th birthday and I needed a pick-me-up.

Instant stardom via an appearance in director Brian De Palma's forthcoming film, *Prince of the City*, was on the auction block at a fund-raising benefit for Friends' Central School, De Palma's *alma mater* and the school my son Steven presently attends. The film would star John Travolta! It had to be a musical extravaganza about life with the Jet Set at Club 54. I was ready to play Jackie Onassis. I had just completed a six week disco course with Jerome.

I hoped to pick up the role at bargain rates, but others were equally frivolous. The bidding zipped to $1900 in seconds. While my superego warned against fiscal indiscretions, my libido sang a serenade about Travolta's preference for older women. My hand shot up of its own accord and stayed up until the prize was mine, and I was $2200 poorer.

The whole package included a day on the set, a night at the Plaza, full make-up and "star treatment," a tantalizing phrase. To me it meant Rita Hayworth, swathed in Blackglama. I hoped De Palma had read the same issues of

Modern Screen while he was growing up. My adoloscent dream of dancing with Fred Astaire was only partial motivation. I had not spent half my life's savings on a whim. I expected to transform my adventures on the silver screen into a warm and amusing book that would make my name a household word.

The following morning, when I picked Steven up at Sunday school, I was one of the sights. One teacher introduced me to her entire class as the woman who was going to be in a movie with John Travolta. Futile years of social climbing were forgotten when I made Joe Dever's column on Monday. He called me Writer Myra Chanin. That was worth $500 at least. My celebrity status had rubbed off on Steven and he was interviewed by his classmates on the bus. For once I had done something that did not mortify him. He even promised to get autographs for all the kids in the class.

My dreams were dealt a mortal blow when Alvin brought home a copy of *Prince of the City* from the library. The prince was no dancer. He was an undercover cop in Brooklyn. How squalid! I quickly revised my fantasies. Since black chiffon was out, I could start eating mayonnaise again, and request a more dramatic role—a fat bag lady with warts.

Composing a letter of introduction to De Palma took me ten days. It had to be brief, but clever. I finally pasted the clipping from Joe Dever's column on my letterhead:

FANTASY: Writer Myra Chanin bid $2,200 on Saturday night for an appearance and star treatment in director Brian De Palma's new film, Prince of the City *to be shot in Manhattan this summer starring John Travolta. She was among the 600 or so who crowded the Ben Franklin Hotel ballroom Saturday night for the Friends Central School's* *first "everything auction." "I write about the collapse of fantasies," said Myra, who seemed jubilant to get started on her newest make believe.*

Underneath I added: When do I report for the love scenes? I enclosed samples of my most amusing writing and waited for an appreciative reply. None came.

In June I read that Travolta was bitten in the face by a dog and had gained 30 pounds. I had still not heard from Fetch Productions and my hysteria made me aggressive. I stopped my coy act and dialed the secret number listed on my gift certificate. Fetch Productions, De Palma's company, was controlled by an answering device that was indifferent to human suffering.

Coldly it recorded my frantic appeals. Obviously my anxiety was deemed detrimental to Brian's mental health. He never called me back. The following week, while I waited for the tone that would once again permit me to vocalize my hysteria, I discovered there was actually another human being on the other end of the line. The recording device treated me with more compassion.

Sam Irvin, Brian's amanuensis, hadn't heard about my co-star's run-in with Fido. Travolta's possible facial scars were the least of Brian's troubles. *Prince of the City* needed another rewrite. Neither financing nor a production date was firm. Travolta was not signed to a contract. They had really auctioned off a pig in a poke.

The most devastating news came last. Irvin didn't know who the hell I was. Hadn't he received my letter or my messages? His recollection was vague. I quickly mailed him another batch of the same material, hoping it would not end up behind some radiator in our Main Post Office. The United States Postal Service has been a major stumbling block in my pursuit of fame. Not only do they lose many of my manuscripts but I am only permitted to receive bills and book offers from Time-Life. Is Martin Bormann working there now and personally censoring Jewish mail, or is the Postmaster General merely attempting to double his revenues by encouraging me to post any ordinary correspondence by Express Mail?

I followed De Palma's every move via the gossip columns. He got married. He began production on a new film, *Dressed to Kill*. Michael Caine and Angie Dickenson would co-star. Some scenes from *Dressed to Kill* would be filmed in Philadelphia at the Museum of Art, an institution that was within walking distance of my house. Although I had paid through the nose for Johnny Baby, to offer me Michael Caine in his stead would have been interpreted by me as a sign of good faith. Perhaps Brian was unaware that I would accept an offer to appear in *Dressed to Kill* as a fulfillment of his obligations to me.

When I called New York again, I was told in whispers that Brian was indeed present, but unavailable to speak to the likes of me. Conversation with ordinary mortals was not on his agenda for that day. He never did call me back.

I had a previous connection with the De Palmas. Brian's father was an orthopedic surgeon who had saved my dad's life when he removed a slipped disc, that was threatening to paralyze him, from his spine. De Palma *père*, was the busiest surgeon in town, but he always found time to calm my mother's fears. How did his son turn out to be such a shit?

I decided to approach Brian from a different angle and called the go-between who had arranged for the prize. I found her in the midst of a depression. She was a true Jewish Princess who just wasn't getting her reward for doing everything right. Her husband had just left her for someone less perfect but more interesting, and his cavalier approach to her requests for money was identical to Brian's reaction to my petitions for recognition.

In October I sent a certified letter to De Palma's bride with a copy of the manuscript of this book. I hoped that sisterhood might forge a bond or that she might be amused into replying to me. I did hear from her. The mailman delivered that little green return card with her signature on it. After that, nothing.

The letters written by the Headmaster of the school were also ignored. Brian and his company came to town and I never heard a word. I checked out the production schedules and discovered that *Prince of the City* was not even on them. I had really been duped!

My husband, Alvin, the reluctant barrister, finally called George Litto, De Palma's producer and got the same runaround until he dropped the word lawsuit. Fred Caruso called Alvin back and was sweet as sugar. The filming in Philadelphia was completed, but there were still some scenes to be shot in New York. Caruso would arrange for me to spend two days watching Brian shoot interiors late in December, and then I could return to New York during the first week in January and do my thing with Angie Dickenson.

We waited, but no one ever called. When Alvin next spoke to Caruso, he had undergone a change of heart. The production company had no obligation to me and De Palma had no time. A few days later I received a letter from the Headmaster. A complete refund was enclosed. They quoted from Sam Irvin's letter to them. "De Palma is no longer set to direct *Prince of the City*. This in itself invalidates the agreement with Mrs. Chanin." Sez who? I don't know where Irvin got his law degree, but I suspect he acquired his legal training from the same place I picked up my medical expertise—in the pages of *Time, Newsweek,* and *Reader's Digest.*

Headmaster Tom Wood added that he thought the refund of my donation would resolve the problem to the best satisfaction of all concerned. It solved nothing to my best satisfaction. I wanted to murder that no-good lying son-of-a-bitch De Palma. Tom Wood was a product of a tradition that requires people to turn the other cheek. I believe that one repays good with good and evil with justice.

Alvin did not jump at the chance to avenge my honor. He prefers less complex litigation like uncontested divorces. I strode around the block to confer with Ben Joseph, Jascha's father. Ben sympathized with my rage and agreed to handle my case. We would sue for breach of contract, tort and punitive damages. I was tempted to try to have de Palma indicted for fraud. He had made a fool out of me. People constantly came up to me on the street with questions about my movie career. I had interest in the story from *Reader's Digest.* Now I had nothing to sell them. What is a relationship with a star worth to a budding writer? About a million bucks. That's the figure I'm suing for.

I also discussed the case with my brother-in-law, Bernie, a senior partner in a respected law firm. I decided to let him handle the preliminary stages of negotiation. His letterhead is more terrifying than that of my original counsel. Four engraved columns list 130 partners. Their names alone cover half of the first page of any correspondence. I suggested he type, "Wise up, Sucker!" on the blank portion of the page and send along with it Polaroid photos of one of the paralegal staff weighing a giant set of interrogatories which the firm normally sends out in any matter they handle.

Bernie will do the work, but he'll sign a different partner's name to the documents. That's so De Palma will know that I'm not just making empty threats. To handle the trial Bernie has selected his favorite associate, a brilliant, tall, self-effacing stutterer who makes the courtroom hang on his every word. I have urged them all to reread *A Merchant of Venice* to prepare for the case. Shylock is a plaintiff after my own heart. De Palma has enraged one of the few people in the United States who won't be bought off with filthy lucre. To understand my point of view, just think about *The Electric Horseman*. I consider myself the Robert Redford of short, fat Jews. De Palma showed as little concern about my feelings as the corporation executives in the movie displayed about the health of their racehorse. Redford stole the horse for the same reason I am suing. To teach a lesson, so that in the future De Palma will think twice before fucking the common man.

More immediate problems must be solved first. My brother-in-law's literary standards impede our progress. Bernie will only mail out absolutely flawless prose. His letter of representation took him three months to compose. It did include the following phrase which I adore:

> "Ms. Chanin has expressed
> admiration for your work
> and regret at being compelled
> to sue you in this matter."

Lines like that are worth the waiting, I suppose, except that Brian reacts to all mailed documents with indifference. I am hoping, however, that efforts typed on parchment paper and delivered personally by a sheriff will break through his reserve.

I hope the complaint is completed before the statute of limitations runs out. It would pain me to resolve my claim against De Palma as damages in a malpractice action against Alvin's only brother.

Either way I'll get to do my performance—on camera or *en camera*. I'm looking forward to showing the jury my emotional distress. That no-good louse will rue the day he threw me off the cast of his picture. He's gonna get really well acquainted with my acting abilities during our month together in Federal Court.

In This Corner,
Wearing the
Purple Apron

Rosemarie Porter's son Eddie and Steven, my preteen crown prince, have been classmates for several years. The first time Steven spent the night with the Porters, he came home with a very alarming report. "Mrs. Porter's a better cook than you are," he announced.

I am, by nature, a very competitive person who happens to be an excellent cook. At that time I ran a small catering business and made desserts for downtown restaurants. I rarely accept Steven's culinary critiques without a grain of salt. He has acquired a taste for imported caviar but sometimes insists on dining at the Pizza Hut.

"What'd she make?" I inquired cynically. "Sloppy Joes and Rice-A-Roni?"

Steven recited a menu suitable for a Roman feast. Black bean soup with choritzos. Homemade pasta with fresh clams. A mocha torte he watched her assemble. She had whipped all the egg whites by hand!

Appearances certainly were deceptive. Rosemarie looked too skinny and chic to be a first-class chef. Her blouses, unlike mine, did not index every sauce that had been stirred in each one. Her countertops were spotless. Her pots were all out of sight. Even at rest, my kitchen looks like Sherman's Army has just finished foraging through it for supplies.

I checked around and learned that Rosemarie also baked for several restaurants and that her training was far superior to mine. She had studied with Beard, Pepin, and Dannen-baum. I had taken five lessons in won ton soup at the Chinatown Y where the instructor apologized more for the policies of Mao Tse Tung than for the consequences of MSG. Still, I was never one to shirk a challenge. I called and asked Rosemarie if Eddie could spend a night with us the following week. Seven days should give me enough time to prepare a four-star meal.

I served him scrumptious baby spareribs that had mari-nated for 72 hours in a divine sauce, and a chickpea and zucchini souffle with FRESH beans, not the canned gunk I sometimes slip to my next of kin. The salad dressing con-tained hazelnut oil, at ten bucks a pint and a 25-year-old sherry vinegar that cost even more. The white raisins in the carrot cake had plumped in brandy. Not just any old brandy. Alvin's last jiggers of Martell's Cordon Blue.

Eddie asked for seconds and thirds while my weight-watching family regarded him with awe. He ate like a vulture but was thin as a rail. Did the Louisiana Hot Sauce, into which he dipped each morsel, rush the nutrients through his intestines too quickly for any to stick to his ribs?

I could tell by the pleased expression on Steven's face that the first round was a draw. A month later Steven slept at his friend's house again. I was waiting on the front steps the following afternoon when the school bus brought him home.

"Well?" I snapped.

"Rack of lamb, broccoli mousse and sweet corn pud-ding." He caught his breath before laying the dessert on me. Homemade mango ice cream.

Shit.

My husband Alvin considered kidnapping Eddie. On

the nights he joined us for dinner Alvin ate like a king. Quenelles. Tempura. Paté en croute. After each four-star dinner Alvin was four pounds heavier.

In March Rosemarie upped the ante and mixed in *minceur* with her *haute cuisine*. Would a normal woman serve veal braised in cream and fresh raspberry sorbet on a Tuesday night! If the Porters dined as sumptuously *en famille* as they did when Steven slept there, only a miracle could explain their deliverance from the gout.

When summer arrived, the boys left for camp. I breathed a sigh of relief and hung up my apron. The Mother Marvelous cook-off had become a real burden to me because I was no longer interested in cooking. A local magazine had just bought my first article and I had turned my baking business over to an unemployed neighbor. I now spent my morning over a hot IBM Selectric typewriter and Alvin was overjoyed when I remembered to salt his frequently served baked chicken parts before I slung them into the stove.

When school opened again in September Steven and Eddie were in different homerooms. Would out of sight mean out of kitchen? Invitations still issued forth from across town, but the boys had conflicting interests. Steven played soccer on Mondays and Wednesday. Eddie took violin lessons on Tuesdays and Thursdays. Music doth have charms.

In October Steven received an invitation to Eddie's birthday bash, an overnight affair that included both dinner and breakfast. I didn't even ask Steven what she served. He told me anyway. Paella and sachertorte for dinner. I forget what she gave them the following dawn.

Steven kept nagging me to invite Eddie over. I suppose he was anxious to dine with the Porters again. I don't blame him. The food she served now beat mine by a mile.

There were still a few leftovers in the back of my freezer that I was saving for special occasions, stews that improved with the passage of time. I was ashamed that my laziness had interfered with my son's relationships. Eddie could visit us until my reserves ran out.

In December the soccer season ended. Eddie was invited to spend Wednesday night with us. I made a mental note to defrost a Moroccan Lamb and Fruit Tangine in the morning, but my memory was jarred by a plethora of rejection slips. My all-time record. Four in one day, including one from *Kosher Home.* To fight my depression I shopped for a dress. When I came home from the mall at four in the afternoon there was a note hanging on my door. Steven and Eddie had walked to the stamp store. Would I please have dinner ready by six.

Dinner! It was still a block of ice! I got back in the car and went shopping. First to McDonald's and then to Carvel's and finally home to do the dastardly deed. I have no problems lying to children. I feel it prepares them for presidential campaigns.

I stripped the Filets-O-Fish bare of their soggy rolls and dribbled a quick mornay sauce on them. I sprinkled tumeric and cumin on the soggy fries and put them both in the oven to keep warm. Into the vanilla custard I mixed chips and nuts and bits of dried fruit and shifted it all into a plastic container that belonged to my unemployed ice cream freezer. I disposed of the printed containers in a neighbor's trash can where a few more fast-food wrappers went undetected among hers. When I set the table I placed a giant size bottle of Tabasco sauce beside Eddie's plate. Mercifully, his taste buds would be out of commission at the start of the meal.

"This is the best fish I ever ate," Eddie declared.

My son agreed. "It's so nice and soft."

They both loved the soggy fries and the tutti-fruiti custard, too. What a fool I had been. Why did I think a child whose mouth was ravaged daily by a tsunami of Tabasco could taste anything at all? Steven's palate was equally coarse. Some gourmets.

I became more bold. I sprinkled Kentucky Fried Chicken with star anise and soy sauce and layered instant puddings in crystal goblets. They lapped it up and made me promise to repeat the very same meal again soon. They had been deprived of preservatives all their lives and took to them like fish to water.

At the next parents' association meeting I tried to avoid Rosemarie but she lay in wait for me at the entrance to the gym. "Eddie says your chicken is just delicious. He could eat it every night."

I accepted her compliments nervously. "It has 11 different spices in it," I mumbled and rushed off to confer with Steven's adviser before Rosemarie asked for the recipe.

Let Rosemarie whip up those hazelnut meringues and slather them in chocolate butter cream. I just transfer viands from paper containers to silver trays. To the boys, it's the way they're presented that counts. They never complain.

The spices I select to doctor up these vittles come from twenty years of reading cookbooks—proof that no knowledge ever goes to waste. From Julia Child and Craig Claiborne I have learned that there's more than one way to cook a goose.

A Daughter of the
Commandments

I joined a synogogue for the first time when I was 41 years old . . . three days after the Arab's Yom Kippur attack. Even a nonbeliever like me felt shocked and threatened by such a sacrilege. It reminded me that a Jew's identification as a Jew is too often determined by his assassin. In the awful event that it did happen here my son Steven's rational protests would prove less convincing than his circumcision. Perhaps my mother was right. Steven should know he is a Jew.

Of course I joined a reform congregation. Even fantasies of extinction could not induce me to sit in the women's section of an Orthodox synogogue or endure interminable hours of Hebrew prayers that I could not read, much less understand. I selected Beth David because I liked the rabbi, Henry Cohen, a witty, unpretentious Texan whose sermons aired out my brains. I had been led back to the fold by Sigmund Freud. The self love that grew out of my analysis heightened my appreciation of the tradition that had produced me. I enrolled Steven in Hebrew school the following year so that tradition might endure.

Last year Steven began to grumble about attending classes when all his friends were playing soccer. "If going to Hebrew school is so terrific why don't you go?" he cried every Thursday afternoon. The ensuing debates were redundant. I won by losing my cool. To me strong-arm victories are hollow triumphs. In order to have justice on my side I joined the adult Hebrew class at Beth David in September.

My parents were cultural rather than observant Jews, more concerned with Marx than Moses. They went to memorial services and said memorial prayers, but sent me to the socialistic Workman's Circle Yiddish schools where so many of the students read on a third grade level that even in junior high we studied literature by listening to the classics read aloud by the teacher. When I graduated I was an expert on Spartacus, but I could barely decipher the headlines in the *Daily Forward*. Would my psychological dyslexia follow me into middle age?

Fortunately, it didn't. Hebrew was easier the second time around. Motivation made a real difference. Each week I copied our classwork into a notebook in script. The vocabulary was familiar from my knowledge of Yiddish. I quickly became teacher's pet. As a late developer, it pleased me to grasp instantly grammatical subtleties that bewildered the doctors in our class and fed my jealous suspicions that most M.D.'s have only enough smarts to master two subjects: the particular organ in which they specialize and the latest I.R.S. rulings on tax shelters.

We progressed through the primer without haste, too easily distracted by Apocrypha. The endless fund of historical anecdotes related by our instructor, David Goldenberg, a talmudic scholar, made me the hit of every dinner party I attended that season. I learned enough Hebrew to help Steven with his homework and we bitterly debated the pronunciation of vowels. Usually we were both wrong, but our ignorance united us.

As Steven's interest improved, so did his grades. His

obsession with his prospective Bar Mitzvah loot diminished as his ambition increased. He asked whether I thought my mother, his Bubbe Tsuni, would actually buy him a car for confirmation.

"Of course she will," I assured him. I have no qualms about lying to children if it will inspire them to excell.

In January I overheard the rabbi ask one of my class-mates whether he had selected a caterer for his Bar Mitzvah. I had just completed an anti-dinner-dance article which decried secular overreactions to religious events. "It's not HIS Bar Mitzvah!" I cried. "It's his son's. These affairs get out of hand because parents confuse the identity of the celebrant!"

Both the rabbi and Bob were nonplussed by my intrusion into their private chat. Common courtesy to a Righteous-ness Expert (me) counts as much as dark of night does to the Postal Service, no deterrent to the performance of our duties.

As usual the Righteousness Expert was wrong. Bob had been discussing the possibility of a belated Bar Mitzvah with the rabbi. Before class was dismissed that morning the rabbi asked us to consider participating in a communal service as a graduation exercise, an adult *B'nai Mitzvot* ceremony to conclude our year of study.

No one had the heart to tell the rabbi we still hadn't learned the entire *aleph bet*. Phonics were far less intriguing than Goldenberg's explanations of the derivation of words. We all understood why heaven was a plural noun in Hebrew, but we were only halfway through *Hasafer*, the Hebrew equivalent of *Fun with Dick and Jane*.

The rabbi misunderstood our silence as a desire for more time to deliberate. He scheduled a meeting the following month for all those in favor. In our congregation no one ever abandons an opportunity to voice an opinion. Even those against the idea showed up for the meeting.

We discussed our reasons for learning Hebrew. Most of the men admitted they felt an obligation to return to the past and fill in the blank left in their lives by the omitted Bar Mitzvah. The women were generally more practical. We had to drive our kids to Sunday school anyway. One guilty soul insisted we had not suffered enough. Another feared our easy success would incite our kids to demand equal treatment. Bar Mitzvah was not a reward for high S.A.T. scores, but a declaration of intention which included a competency test.

When Henry asked for a show of hands only five took the plunge. Two men, two women and me. My reason really stunned him. I thought it would make him happy.

We took additional instruction from the cantor, translated prayers and learned those "golden oldies," the Torah blessing chants. When the cantor divided the service I volunteered to read a prayer that had terrified me a few weeks earlier, the first time I saw how difficult it was. The Torah reading was divided in five parts as well. We each got two commandments. Was it pure chance that my assignment included the one I broke most frequently? Honor *my* mother! Impossible. Even long life is a paltry reward for such self-sacrifice. My mother is a manipulative widow who frequently confuses independence and hostility.

We did a dry run at a children's service and got good reviews from our kids. While I stood on the platform I glanced into the actual Torah scrolls for the first time. No one had ever told me there would be no vowels! I recognized a few words and breathed easier until I realized that none of the familiar words were included in my particular Torah portion.

The Righteousness Expert lived up to her title when the time came to make up the guest list. No business associates. No social obligations. Only people to whom I felt close. I hadn't seen my mother's relatives in ten years. They were not invited. My late father's family are observant Jews who take pride in their obscure connection to the *Bal Shem Tov*. (His grandson adopted my grandfather.) They would appreciate my efforts and my mother might even receive a few reflected glory points. As the nonconformist in the bunch, the college dropout who didn't get married till she was 33, I got a warm feeling from just imagining their approval and I realized there were reasons for my decision that I had not revealed to myself.

After I finished daydreaming about my flawless performance, I pictured the party afterward. Oh, shit! Could the Righteousness Expert serve store-bought cakes to her near and dear? Not when they knew she was the former Mother Wonderful who had once baked desserts for gain. After two nights of listening to my mixer rattle, the Righteousness Expert found an honorable solution. I ordered cheesecakes from the woman I had trained to assist me, who was now in business for herself.

There was still one fly in the ointment. I was displeased with the name of the ceremony. At my age I was no daughter of anything. I demanded a service for Women of the Commandments who, like me, had chosen Judaism in midlife. Henry just smiled and ignored my requests. Had I overrated him? Was tact more important to him than truth?

My mother, my role model, set high stubbornness standards, and when I was commissioned by a local newspaper to describe the event, I entitled my article "A Woman of the Commandments," and because my deadline was three weeks before the service, faked the ending. The final paragraph included a feminist polemic describing my extrication from roles I had been programmed to play and hinted at my dissatisfaction with a faith that insisted on considering grown women still as daughters. The Righteousness Expert rides again!

That night the sanctuary was packed and we were letter perfect. Bob said *b'mishretayhem* correctly, a real test even for Jewish lips. He read the final commandment which included the admonition against coveting your neighbor's property. He told me later that he had ordered a plaque made of that Hebrew phrase to present to his law partner, who handled shopping-center acquisitions.

After we sat down, Henry announced that ours was the first Bar/Bat Mitzvah he ever attended where the children had pleasure from their parents, and from the front row, Steven beamed in agreement. In his sermon, Henry spoke about our search for meaning in our lives and suggested that the search itself was the answer. In his view, all Jewish roots converge in the soil of Mt. Sinai where Moses was given the laws we had read earlier in the Torah.

As the guests filed out I stood beside Henry and embraced friends and strangers. Everyone seemed moved. Me too. My family decided that kissing me took precedence over grabbing some sweets and waited in line to greet me, a decision some quickly regretted. There were not enough chairs for the overflow crowd, and my cousin Milton had an anxiety attack. Would the triple chocolate cheesecake be all gone before he found a fork? I pointed to the kitchen and told him to fend for himself. I was the Bat Mitzvah, not the hostess.

From the corner of my eye I watched my mother take advantage of this infrequent opportunity to revel in my reflected glory. With tears in their eyes, she and my Aunt Della agreed that it was sad that my father had not lived to see me reading from the Torah. My father was an obsessive compulsive Marxist who celebrated Yom Kippur, our annual fast day, by a nonstop feast. Had he become a believer since his demise?

During the ride home I explained my reluctance to be called a Bat Mitzvah to Steven, and he and I discussed how relationships must change to endure. As he becomes more independent I must relinquish my veto power over his actions, or suffer the consequences of his resentment.

My mother sat in the back of the car and boiled at the very idea of such inconstancy. Why did her daughter have to be such a nut? Della's children couldn't do enough for their mother. They drove her everywhere, even food shopping. Unlike me, my mother had never listened to Della's perfect daughters-in-law gleefully plan Della's funeral.

"A mother is still a mother . . ." she sighed and when no one agreed with her, switched to a more responsive track. She had heard several people comment on my article, the second one I had ever sold. Where could she buy it?

I asked Alvin to stop at our house so I could give her the copy I had saved for her.

"She can read it tomorrow," he snapped. "I have to walk Spot and I'm tired. I don't feel like driving around all night taking people home!"

My mother only lives two blocks from us. What was the reason for Alvin's short fuse? His stomach bulged out over his belt, an indication he had once again lost control around the mocha tortes.

"I'll drive her home. You go to sleep," I retorted.

"You don't have to bother," my mother whined, in her element at last. "I don't want to give anybody trouble."

Why didn't that phrase set off warning bells? Her speciality is creating disasters when she's only trying to help. I asked her to wait in the car. I would get the newspaper and drive her right home. Did she follow that simple request? Are you kidding? When I came to the door, I saw her sitting on the sidewalk.

Blood trickled down her leg. Could she have hurt herself so badly tripping on a brick pavement? Not ordinarily, but she had hit a metal valve cover and gashed her knee to the bone.

Was it my imagination or did a victorious smile flash across her face? "I'll walk home," she announced. "I don't want to bother you," she repeated. As usual her words belied her actions.

My claims of independence are nonsense. How can anyone escape such determined love? What other occupation does she have beside setting traps for me? She always wins in the end.

Who helped her into the house? A Woman of the Commandments? Don't make me laugh. Her daughter washed off the cut and drove her to the emergency ward. Her daughter flipped through ripped *Good Housekeepings* until the staff finished their coffee break and deigned to sew up her cut. I did not hear, but I know that her fellow patients were told that her daughter had driven her to the hospital and waited outside to take her home. A more embellished version would be related the following morning to my Aunt Della.

Whose fault was it that she cut her knee? Entirely mine. I

could have waited to give her a copy of my article. Instead I jumped at the chance to give my Mommy pleasure, and my claims of separation from her are absurd. I am linked to her by love and rejection and time. Woman of the Commandments, indeed. I am ashamed of my pretentions. I'm still more of a daughter than I like to believe.

A Fiend in Utero

Sonya, my mother, claimed I was evil from the very moment of my conception. I kicked and would not let her sleep. I made her vomit. I bound up her bowels and forced her into a lifelong dependency on lemon juice and prunes.

Instead of becoming a daughter who loved Sonya as she had loved her mother, I copied the side of her nature that was buried under her fears. Sonya's need to appear ordinary was understandable. In the world into which she had been born, to be noticed was to beg for death.

When Sonya was seven, she and her younger brothers, Aaron and Seymour, were flung down cellar steps by Cossacks. They waited there to be shot. Furniture crashed over their heads. Drunken laughter veiled the screams of Uncle David when the murderers ripped off his beard. They dragged him through the village to be mocked and forgot the children who clung to each other in the dark and wept over their impending fate.

When Sonya was ten, she and Aaron and Seymour smuggled butter into Odessa and traded it on the black market for sugar and tea. They wrapped their merchandise in stained newspapers secured with knotted string. Death would have been the reward for discovery, but they were brazen and clever, three children who huddled together on the wooden benches of the third-class carriage. Their legs fluttered like twigs in the wind and shrouded the precious bundles hidden under the seats.

Where are they now?

Aaron is dead. Seymour is a family outcast. Sonya sits amid glistening crystal on the 18th floor of a hi-rise and leads me into the past. I have heard these legends of her childhood so often I can recite them with her. "I was *die Mama's* favorite. She did more for me than for anybody else. Something was wrong with my arm. *Die Mama* took me to Odessa to bathe in special springs there so I wouldn't be crippled. We were very poor. I don't know where she got the money, but I'll never forget what she did for me!"

Die Mama's grave is carpeted with forget-me-nots. Who will plant flowers on Sonya's grave? She took me to bathe in waters, but I am not grateful. On summer afternoons after my romp under the sprinklers at Crup's Garage, she carried me across Seventh Street wrapped in towels. I was six, I weighed 80 pounds and I had been crippled by her.

"Where I lived they didn't let Jewish girls in the high school, so *die Mama* found teachers and I studied at home. I was very good in school. I knew all five books of Caesar by heart!" Sonya's eyes flash. The sunlight makes her white hair glitter like tinsel. She is a handsome woman, tiny and vain. "Sometimes I can't remember where I put my keys and other times faces from long ago come before my eyes, so clear, like I saw the people yesterday. I see his face, the Latin teacher. I even remember his name. To remember a name from so long ago!" She searches my face for approval.

"What was his name?" I hope my memory will be as good.

"Greenstein. He was a very good teacher, but he was a drunkard. *Die Mama* had to give him something to drink or he would leave without giving me a lesson. On the coldest days, when we didn't have a piece of bread in the house for ourselves, *die Mama* ran from house to house until somebody gave her enough schnapps so Greenstein would stay and teach me Latin." Sonya sighs. *Die Mama. Die Mama. Still die Mama.* Gitel Katz has been buried for 40 years, but Sonya is a faithful child. Each September she trudges on three buses to visit *die Mama's* grave.

"When I went to Odessa to take the examinations, I got the highest marks. I graduated for pharmicist when I was fourteen, and the tests in Russia are not like here. There when you graduate you know something. I smuggled butter when I was ten years old. Ten-year-old children here, what do they know? In Russia we were adults already by then!"

For the next year Sonya deciphered physicians' scribbles. She ground roots into powders and filled bottles with potions. She was clean and compulsive. Everything had to be done right. It was a good year for her. The Cossacks were fighting the Bolsheviks in the north and her town was peaceful. Sonya could go anywhere and not be afraid. A year later war broke out and Sonya became a nurse in the World War I Russian Army.

What! *Die Mama* allowed them to conscript her darling! Why hadn't *die Mama* ripped off her arm and driven away the recruiters in a sea of blood? Sonya ignores my question, because there is no answer. The story of *die Mama's* failure has been edited by Sonya.

The holes in time absorb me. I am more intrigued by what Sonya omits than I am by what she reveals.

"In the war they gave us two pounds of bread a day, in the morning. That was all. I tried to eat a little bit and save the rest for nighttime, but I was always so hungry I gobbled down whatever they gave me and then I didn't have food for the rest of the day. I used to think that if I could just have enough to eat for one whole day I wouldn't ask for anything else from life."

Sonya is a widow. Now she eats almost nothing. "After all, who wants to bother cooking for just one person. I have to be careful what I eat. My stomach is funny. I go out for lunch, but not because I'm hungry. I get crazy sitting in the apartment by myself all the time. In Wanamaker's I always find somebody to talk to. It's very lonely here," she whines.

"You don't have to be alone. Mrs. Stein. Rose. The Heller sisters. You could invite them over for dinner."

"I should just be like you. Feed the world and everybody is your friend. It's not so bad yet that I have to buy people with meals."

Sonya is alone because she will not compromise. She doesn't want friendship. All she wants is my love. I wander into her kitchen and open the refrigerator door. Sonya uncovers caches of cookies. "Here, try this. Just taste it. I made them because you said you would be here. I made it special for you!"

I become an infant and let her feed me. She clings to the baby in me.

In the war Sonya trembled in a shack and plugged up veins. Battles crept closer until they were upon her. Bombs blasted out craters around her wagon. The canvas roof over her head blazed up. Sonya and Birdie, another nurse, stumbled through smoke and raced toward the forest. Birdie faltered. Her slimy fingers slipped away.

"We worked side by side in the wagon. She was a good friend to me. She fell back on the ground and I didn't even stop to see if I could help her." Sonya reveals an ancient guilt, the tip of an iceberg. She does not describe the joy she felt when she realized Birdie rather than she had been chosen to die.

"A man came at me and Alvin with a gun last year."

"What did you do?"

"I ran away."

"You ran away and left Alvin!" Sonya is outraged that I deserted my husband.

"Of course I ran. Anybody would run! Alvin would have run too, except that I saw the gun first!"

"Why are you screaming?" Sonya whimpers. "What did I say that was so terrible. I only asked if you left Alvin. You said that yourself." She defends herself in deceptive tones. "And Alvin. What did he do?"

"He stood there and the man walked right by him. Alvin's lucky. He'll live forever."

Sonya laughs nervously. She waited a long time for me to get married. She dislikes Alvin but she loves having a son-in-law.

"People think they'll be heroes, but that's bullshit. They'll save their own asses, just like we did."

Sonya frowns. Where did I learn such language? Not from her lips. My behavior confuses her. Am I a changeling? The flesh of her flesh should be perfect.

I stopped running at the corner, but Sonya never stopped. Was she captured or did she surrender? Did peasants slake their lust on her? Omissions. The past rushes by like pages of time in a film and then Sonya appears in a hospital for prisoners in Poland.

The stench of acid filled her nostrils. A wimple imprisoned her hair. Gangrene and hemorrhages colored her days as she carried basins across concrete floors, sponged the wounded and cheered mustard-gassed serfs with lies.

She transcribed letters for men without fingers. She wiped away pus. She was a good nurse, kindest to me when I was the most dependent. She read me funny stories and acted out the scenes so well that I giggled through high fevers. Whenever Dr. Isenberg approached my ears with his wicked lances, she veiled my eyes with embroidered handkerchiefs. My cries never alarmed her. The screams of dying men had made her grateful for my tiny wails.

Before the war Sonya had been a vegetarian; at home *die Mama* had baked eggplant mousses and mushroom cutlets for her, proud that her Sonya refused to have innocent creatures killed on her behalf. *Die Mama's* kitchen was spotless. The hospital kitchen was dirty. Sonya suspected she was being fed horsemeat. She developed strange theories about food and disease. She ate less and less and was always exhausted.

One of the doctors in the hospital befriended her and forced her to stop behaving like a fool. No one was trying to poison her. "It's very bad when somebody knows a little bit and thinks she knows a lot," he chided her. His words were engraved on her brain. They have supplied a lifetime of ammunition against me.

"There's plenty to eat in this world without shedding blood," Sonya insists as she picks at eggs and cottage cheese. "I eat some chicken now and then, but not often. I still remember the geese at home running through the yard without heads." She cringes. "It's a shame for the animals. They want to live too. We're still savages who kill just to fill our bellies."

"Death supports life," I reply, but Sonya prefers to speak about survival.

The same doctor arranged to have Sonya transferred to a orphans' home on the outskirts of Warsaw, where she taught the children to sew and embroider. "He was very good to me. After all, what was I to him? Another person wouldn't have cared about me, but he was a very fine type. He liked me very much."

"Was he married?" I long for romance.

"What kind of a question is that? I worked for him. He was an old man," Sonya replies impatiently.

"What was his name?"

"Go remember a name from so long ago. He was tall with red hair and a long nose. A face like a horse. Big, white teeth." Sonya squints as though hoping to sharpen her memory. Suddenly she looks up. "Dr. Orchney. See. How do you like that?"

"Was he Jewish?"

"In Poland she wants a Jewish doctor to be in charge of a hospital. We were lucky they let us have Jews to do the circumcisions."

On two sepia photographs, their corners rotting with time, Sonya, encased in a thick wool cardigan, towers over the orphans in her charge. Her hair is twisted into a bun on the nape of her neck. She has delicate skin and an earnest expression. Young, solemn and very pretty. She does not smile.

Five levels of orphans pose on a staircase as wide as the porch of the summerhouse behind them. Sonya shows two girls how to make French knots like the ones she embroidered on my carriage cover. Four boys with shaved heads embrace their sewing machines, the boots poised to march on the treadles.

"I loved those children just like they were my own," she assures me. Did she oppress their lives with the same unconscious malevolence she heaped on me, her true child? She and I shouted our differences at each other, while my father, a frightened creature for whose love I vainly battled, played with invoices and checks, pretending to be a businessman.

"*Die Mama* thought I was dead. I thought they were killed in the war, but they were on their way to America from Russia. *Die Mama* met my cousin on the street in War-saw one afternoon. He told her I was alive. When my cousin told me that my family was in Warsaw I fainted away. Then everything happened so fast. One minute I was teaching the children, and the next minute I was kissing them good-bye."

The principal gave Sonya a valise. Her cousin sent a wagon to take her to the station. She was to meet *die Mama* beside the train to Hamburg and she was not to worry about anything. *Die Mama* had tickets and a passport for her. Everything would be all right.

The children pulled at her skirts. "Sonya, Sonya," they cried. "Take me with you, please, please. Take me to America."

A fat driver with stains on his coat pulled Sonya up the footholds to the seat in the front of the wagon. He clicked his tongue and the horse lumbered toward the gate. The children marched beside the wagon, calling Sonya's name. Sonya turned to wave good-bye but she could hardly see. Tears poured down her cheeks and soaked her collar.

"It was dark when the driver left me off at the depot. I was so afraid. Suppose my cousin had made a mistake. Suppose they had already left. What would I do then?"

Sonya looked through the wrought iron arch. In the distance she saw a signboard that said WARSAW-BERLIN-HAMBURG. Steam poured out of the chimney of the train beside the sign. Were they leaving without her?

Sonya ran toward the track. Her suitcase banged against her leg. A tall man in a greatcoat paced back and forth beside the waiting room. His fur collar was turned up to protect his neck from the cold. His hands were clasped behind his back and the brim of his cap cast a long shadow over his face. When he turned the headlight of the locomotive revealed the face of my grandfather Max.

Sonya screamed, *"Daddy! Daddy!"* and ran into his arms.

Sonya's eyes mist and she is silent. I cry too each time I hear this tale. Her father embraces her. The waiting room door swings open and *die Mama*, Aaron, Seymour and Yetta all rush out and envelop her in love. "I cried and they cried. Everybody who was there cried," Sonya laughs. "I don't think there was a dry eye in the whole station that day."

Such a loving man, my grandfather Max. Why is he a phantom? Did he exist only to swing Sonya in the air? The reunion is his cameo appearance in Sonya's autobiography. He was a tall, slender man with a Vandyke beard and meticulous linen. His work was insignificant. He served as a model for a whole generation of failures.

He loved vaudeville and schmaltz herrings, and attended Saturday matinees instead of going to synogogue. He brought ripe fish to snack on during the intermissions and tapped his feet to the music. Max died before I was born and I was named for him.

His memory haunts me. *"Daddy! Daddy!"* I cry. He swings me into the air and presses me against his heart. My father worked from dawn to dusk packing spices into cellophane bags. He never touched me. Sonya worked by his side. She now has enough money to pay for a decade in a first class nursing home whenever her morbid fantasies are fulfilled and cancer strikes her.

America.

"For the first year I was here, I didn't stop crying. I lost maybe forty pounds."

"Why?"

"I don't know. I couldn't eat. I missed Russia."

"You missed smuggling butter? You missed the pogroms? You missed running for your life?"

"It was more than that. I knew where everything was. I went to lectures and concerts. I had interesting friends."

"There were concerts here too. Opera. Friends . . ." Did this isolated woman who needs constant approval ever have any friends?

"They treated me with respect there. I was a pharmacist. I was a teacher. What was I here? Another girl who worked in a sweatshop."

"You could have gone back to school."

"I didn't have any money."

"How much did it cost?"

"It didn't cost anything," she admits. "To be a pharmacist here I would have to go to night school for a year."

"That's not a long time. Why didn't you go?"

"What do you know about what it was like in those days!" Sonya attacks me. "I didn't have an easy life. Sometimes I can't believe I went through what I did and still lived. My father didn't make very much money. We all had to help out *die Mama*.

"In the shop where I worked they liked me so much that the boss paid me even in the slack times so I wouldn't work for somebody else. Men didn't make as much money as I did, and I held on to it. I had five thousand dollars in the bank when I got married."

Sonya hemmed overcoats and appliqued wedding gowns. Tiny hand stitches. How many tears did she shed for each dollar? How much boredom did she endure? Am I unfair? Sonya broached a new land. She faced a strange language. Still there were others who grappled with the same terrors and have more than bankbooks to show at the ends of their lives. I judge Sonya by the same standards with which she has always judged me. I also demand perfection.

"Maybe I was foolish to cry like that for so long," she admits to a minor fault. Did she think she could manipulate fate as easily as she could control *die Mama*?

"Why did you stop crying?"

"I just made up my mind. There was a man in the shop with me . . ." The love theme begins. "He liked me very much. He explained things to me. If it wouldn't be for him, I don't know what I would have done. He was a very intelligent person." A journalist marking time in the factory until he could get a job on a newspaper.

"Orenstein?"

Sonya nods. First love in a new world. A man with no first name or initials. No photographs. Just a voice who explained things. A memory. A myth.

Did she touch him? Did his body ever shield her from the cold? Did they explore unfamiliar sensations in the dark? I deny Sonya's sexuality, just as she has always denied mine.

"He liked me very much."

"And you?"

Sonya twists the engagement ring my father gave her. "He had a sweetheart in Poland. He promised her he would bring her to America. How could I let him break a promise to a girl who waited for him? It would always be on my conscience that because of me that girl would be unhappy. You can't build happiness on somebody else's misery. I told him he should marry her." She stares into my eyes, proud of her self-denial.

"And did he marry her?"

"I think so."

"Are they still together?"

"I don't know. He moved to Canada."

"Did he ever write about you?"

"What was there to write?"

"Did he ask you to go to Canada with him?"

"It was so long ago. Who remembers?"

"You couldn't marry him because you would have to leave *die Mama.*"

My remark enrages her. "What are you talking about? How could I marry a man who had a sweetheart already?"

The light filters through the blinds and casts long shadows on the rug. Sonya switches on a lamp with a white silk shade. All the furnishings are white or gold. Some of them are 20 years old, but everything looks new. Her apartment is like the display window of a store. She shows it to strangers so they can admire her, but she rarely invites anyone to stay. Friendships are difficult for her because she demands adoration. "I have my pride. I didn't like the way the Heller sisters talked to me last week."

"What did they say?"

"They said what they said. I'm just as educated as they are. I'm just as smart, and if they don't like me, let them go with somebody else. I don't need them to put me down."

Sonya has acquired a snazzy vocabulary from Johnny Carson, but her attitudes revert to the days at home. She must be loved as uncritically as *die Mama* loved her, or she sulks in her room and sews dresses for herself out of expensive remnants. She attends a current events class two mornings a week. When she gets all dressed up strangers stop her on the street to admire her outfits. She washes all her own dresses and irons them herself. On Thursday she moves her furniture and scrubs the woodwork and the walls.

"I know how to take care of things so they last," she announces, distressed by my low housekeeping standards. "A person always has to think about tomorrow." She quotes a Yiddish proverb to support her. Sonya pulls proverbs from four languages whenever we disagree. The wisdom of the past is always on her side, except that I do not care who is right. I just go my own way.

"When I got married, your father didn't have a job. It was a good thing I had money saved. We needed it until he found the business."

Enter, Lew, my beloved. A delicate man with a large memory and a tiny ego. He had the face of an angel and fine hair that was beginning to thin. On their wedding portrait his hands clasp the sides of a frock that Sonya beaded. He looks boyish, timid, innocent. Sonya's hair is marcelled. Her right hand is propped against her hip. In her white satin shoes she is taller than he. She looks belligerent and demanding. Would anyone else see all this, or will I always be jealous?

Three snapshots record their honeymoon. They sit on a ridge around the flower beds of the Hotel Dennis in Atlantic City. A lamppost divides them. Lew looks disappointed and Sonya looks grim. Was he inexperienced and gentle or nervous and cruel? Would it have mattered? Sonya was into dominance and dirt. A douchebag hung on the door. Lysol was her aphrodisiac. She scrubbed the bathtub in the suite first and then she scrubbed herself out afterward. Let her be frigid. Why should he find warmth in her?

Sonya and Lew rented an apartment eight blocks away from *die Mama's* house. Even that was too far away. Sonya had to visit *die Mama* every night. She cried until Lew took her over in a taxi. Eight weeks later they moved into *die Mama's* house. The movers carried the new cherrywood bedroom suite up three flights of stairs to Sonya's old room. *Die Mama* slept alone in the adjoining room. Sonya stopped crying and went back to work. Lew looked around for a business.

He bought a candy store, and spent two years among penny candy and petty thieves, terrified of the toughs who made obscene gestures at him through the glass. Lew tried to discuss evolution with the driver who delivered the ice cream. His customers took advantage of his love of books and stole candy while he read Spinoza. He sold the store at a loss, took five hundred dollars and went into the wholesale grocery business with his brother Carl. Sonya was pregnant with me, a fetus who gave her no peace and made her retch twice a day. She was dizzy and exhausted and terrified of motherhood. *Die Mama* was there. Her sister Yetta lived around the corner. They would help. They had to. Sonya was afraid to pick me up. She was certain I would fall out of her arms and shatter like a china plate. Yetta and *die Mama* washed and diapered me during the first few months of my life, while Sonya boiled my diapers.

My father rose at four A.M. and crept out of the house. He drove his rented truck down to his father's house and hauled cartons along dim hallways, getting the truck ready to go out with the day's orders. Carl was the salesman. He could entice store owners to buy more than they wanted, but he could not remember prices. My father never forgot anything, but he could not relate to the customers. My father was jealous of Carl's charm. Carl envied Lew's intelligence. They were incompatible in every other way.

Carl was dirty. My father showered every night. Carl gambled and drank. My father was a puritan. My father longed for peace. Carl was always angry. He suffered at home because his wife would not allow him in her bed. Carl was afraid of his wife and he took out his rage on my father.

Lew was timid and honest. Carl was a born crook. He climbed out fire exits in hotels and stiffed restauranteurs. He bought "hot" merchandise. Cases of canned goods that toppled off shipping platforms rolled over to Carl's doorstep.

"I don't care how cheap it is," my father screamed. "I don't want to go to prison on account of your bargains!"

"They don't put you in prison for 12 cans of soup. They put you in prison for murder!" Carl yelled back.

The fights endured until my father died. There were other problems too. Carl could not be trusted to hold money overnight. Even though my father was done with his work at three in the afternoon, he paid bills and ordered merchandise and waited for Carl to turn over the day's receipts. It was always dark when Lew pulled up in front of *die Mama's* brownstone. He hung his jacket in the hall, his head still ringing with Carl's curses.

Where was Lew's wife? She was ironing my dresses in the basement. *Die Mama* waited for him in the kitchen. Pots steamed when she removed the lids. Fresh vegetables. Savory stews.

"Want more?" *die Mama* asked. She spoke no English.

Before he could demur, she had ladled more into his dish.

No time for Darwin. No time for Spinoza. Time to count the money and add up the sales slips, write up the deposit and go upstairs. On his way to bed my father passes my room. Does he stop? Maybe. I am already asleep. Even if I had been awake he would not have been permitted to touch me. He was dirty. Covered with germs.

We live in a three story brownstone surrounded by mohair upholstery and antimacassars. The smell of garlic drifts in from the iron kettle filled with brisket and potatoes that always simmers on the stove in the summer kitchen.

Sonya arranges bottles in a primitive autoclave. She did not nurse me because her tit would not fit in the sterilizer.

My carriage stands beside the back door. The sun shines on me. When I wake and cry, my nurse Yetta comforts me. She dotes on me, grateful for any excuse to escape from a husband she despises. Yetta feeds me my gruel. Yetta whoops me in the air and teaches me how to laugh.

Later I lurch down Franklin Street with Sonya and *die Mama* on either side of me. Each one supports me so that I look like I am walking unaided even though I am only eight months old. I was toilet trained when I was ten months old and I sang Russian songs at my first birthday party. When I was two I recited narrative poems in Yiddish. I was a merry child, smart and a bit willful. When Sonya discovered she was pregnant again, she had an abortion.

"I don't know why they make such a fuss about it on the television. We did it too. I went to a doctor's office and when I left it was over."

"Why didn't you want another child?"

"I thought I wouldn't have enough to give two children everything."

Where did I learn that my isolation was a consequence of my black heart?

"And," Sonya adds. "You were very bad. You wouldn't listen to me and you were a terrible eater."

A terrible eater! Photographs belie her words. Tree trunk thighs crease full skirts. Scalloped collars accent my chins. Still not fat enough. *Die Mama* fills triangular blintzahs with eggs and cream cheese for me and stuffs chicken necks with noodle pudding. She laces up her oxfords and trudges to an A&P where only strangers will see her buy non-kosher bacon for me.

Meals become rituals with Sonya as the high priestess. The spoon high in the air where I will not notice it. I am not hungry, but I will eat. Her left hand steadies a bowl of steaming soup. She begins the litany. "Eddie Cramer's nose was dripping when he knocked on my door." Sonya describes a dirty boy who lived in back of us.

When I open my mouth to laugh the spoon unloads its contents on my tongue.

"Do you know what he wanted?"

I know. He wanted my soup.

"Doesn't your mother make soup?" Sonya asked the phantom supplicant.

"She only gives me soup from cans."

Sonya and I grimace together. No need to hide the spoon any more. Scheherazade has entrapped me once again. "Go way, Eddie Cramer. Gerareе! This soup is not for you. This soup is just for my daughter."

My lips open wide and Sonya feeds me into freakhood. I become fatter and they tell me I am beautiful. Has Sonya learned anything from the past? No. My Steven laughs at the same story. The chicken soup is now for him. Eddie Cramer, Sonya has turned you into an eternal beggar pleading for liquid gold. Not for you the soups, the roasts, the chickens. Sonya's food must insure the survival of her issue. Sonya herself eats almost nothing. Perhaps she shares her own dinner with Eddie Cramer.

By the time I was four I looked like an inflated plastic doll. Too fat for chubbies now, Sonya sews all my clothes. Pleated plaid skirts and peasant blouses embroidered with cross-stitch roses. Fancy finishing.

I slide down the sandstone incline beside our front steps. Grime soils my underpants. Dirt streaks my thighs. Why did

I roll in filth when Sonya loved cleanliness? The only time she touched me was when she bathed me.

I recline in the bathtub and read comics while Sonya kneels on the black and white tile bathroom floor. She lifts my leg and rinses the soap off it. I put it back in the water.

"The other . . ."

I permit her to wash that one as well, and then lean forward so she can scrub the rest of me. When I stand up she wraps me in a towel and dries me off. She holds out my underpants so I can step into them. She buttons my dress. Sonya is a wonderful servant, and I refuse to obey her.

I laugh when she lunges at me with her outstretched hand. Who is she to discipline me? *Die Mama* will not permit it. Hit the child, the girl, her darling! Sonya might just as well try to hit the Messiah. I hide behind *die Mama's* skirts protected by the billowing shield of her flesh.

"Don't hit the child!" *die Mama* commanded. Sonya was a better daughter than I was. She obeyed.

Die Mama could not stop Sonya's curses, cries as old as time. "God should only send you a child like you are. I never had any more children because I was afraid I would have another devil like you. You were always bad, even before you were born!" A fiend in utero. I laugh at her but somewhere deep in my heart I begin to believe that I am capable of any evil.

"Bruce was raised without a father, and look how good he is to Della," she needles me even today. I am fatherless too. "Della didn't even know where he was half the time." Lucky Bruce. I was guarded as closely as the crown jewels.

When I play in the street, *die Mama* spies on me through the lace curtain. She has yellow skin and features like an Indian. She is a faithful sentry. Only she understands how the Angel of Death swoops down on the unsuspecting.

Die Mama taps on the pane. Her lips beseech me to remain on the pavement. When I cross the street she runs to the door. "The trolleys! They'll kill you!" she calls to me in Yiddish. Did she fear my death or did she long for it? Did she suspect I had outgrown her desperate adoration?

She smelled foreign. She looked inappropriate. She fed me lies. I looked strange and I wanted to be like everyone else. Everyone else spoke English. No one lived with a grandmother who dogged them and begged them not to leave her.

"Go away! Leave me alone!" I cried, but she paid no attention. She knew more than I did. Only she could save me from death. Perhaps. But she could not save herself.

Sonya wants to die like *die Mama* did, in a coma for weeks, surrounded by children changing her dressings like a staff of trained nurses. It was too late. *Die Mama* had delayed the surgery too long. Other things were more important. The house needed painting. The facade was preserved.

In the shadow of the valley of death, *die Mama* called my name in a Yiddish litany. "The child! The child! Don't go in the street! The trolleys, they'll kill you!"

Sonya took me to the hospital in a taxi. The smell of disinfectant overwhelmed me. I tried not to breathe but I could not shut out my fears. Why was I here?

"Is this the child?" the nurse asked.

Sonya nodded. I was their last hope.

They led me into a room where bottles hung upside down around a bed. A thin wheezing sound fluttered from a cellophane canopy over the head of the bed. Sonya lifted me up and stood me on a stool on the right of the plastic tent. *Die Mama! Die Mama!* She was almost as white as the sheets that covered her body. Her toothless mouth was a puckered hole. Egg whites dripped into her down through tubes that disappeared under the sheets.

She whispered my name. "Don't go in the street."

"Talk to her," Sonya hissed. "She'll die if you don't save her. Tell her you'll never go into the street again. Tell her to open her eyes and live."

Never go into the street again! Never cross the street again!

"Save her!" Sonya wept. "Save her!"

How could I save her? A six-year-old child who never did anything right. A fount of evil? How could I become a good angel now?

"I'm here," I whispered in Yiddish. "I'm not in the street. Get well and I'll never cross the street again." Empty words poured from my mouth. I loved her but the price was too high.

The nurse took pity on me and led me into the hall.

"*Nu?*" Yetta asked.

Sonya bursts into tears. "I'll bring her tomorrow. We'll try again."

"No!" my Uncle Seymour shouts. "Don't be a fool. She's dying. Why are you doing this to the child?"

Two days later *die Mama* called my name for the last time. Her death left me with the belief that I had magic powers. A fiend in utero. She died because I did not wish to save her. How could a child so evil save anyone.

I was denied the chance to mourn. I went to the movies with my cousin Bruce. I did not watch the casket being lowered. I did not see Sonya try to fling herself into the grave. Because I did not see her in death, for me, *die Mama* still lives. It would have helped me to stand beside *die Mama's* coffin and cry.

"How can you talk to Sonya?" my eleven-year old son Steven asks.

"She didn't do it on purpose. Who knows what awful things she was told." I defend her now that my evil powers were dispelled by a wizard who dared me to kill him. How can I explain to Steven the benefits of the spell. To be able to kill is to be able to create. The evil was the source of my imagination. My omniscience was the base of my passion.

"When I was ten I smuggled butter into Odessa," Sonya chants her tale.

"When Steven was ten he built rockets that flew."

"I don't say what I did is better," she backs off. "I only said it was different."

She lies. She believes that smuggling butter is better than building rockets, that saving for cancer is better than paying a maid, that unhappiness is superior to joy and that she is better than I am. Perhaps she is. She survived terrors that were created by history. My fears were self-inflicted, but does that make them easier to endure.

She placates me now because she needs me to stage her death. "I want to pay for perpetual care for *die Mama's* grave and for mine and Lew's too." She glares at me. When the azaleas wither will I replace them? Will I visit her remains. I may be a better daughter than I dream I am.

"And if I get like Aaron was, where I don't know who I am, I don't want to lay in wet sheets. I want to go to a good nursing home. That's why I saved all my life. Put that in my will," she orders Alvin.

"That doesn't go into a will," he replies. "A will describes what to do with your money after you die, not while you're dying."

She does not hear. "And if I get like Yetta where they

can't do anything to make me well again, if I'm unconscious for years, I want you to promise that you'll keep me alive. I don't want them to pull the plug. Even if I'm a vegetable I want to live as long as I can. Promise me you'll do that," she begs.

"I will."

"See," she giggles, embarrassed at having revealed herself even to me. I'm an old lady and I'm still not ready to die."

She lies. She has lived to die from the time she was flung into the cellar. Who knows what sacrifice she offered to destiny so that her life might be spared, while she stood in the dark with her brothers and waited to be shot.

The Passionate Shopper

The Pleasure Chest, Philadelphia's only Love Boutique, is a spotless bazaar of erotica located on the ground floor of a midtown brownstone. The shop serves mostly straight, middle-class folks who would like to extend their sexual parameters. People like you and me, our friends and neighbors, perhaps even our relatives, could conceivably drop in to titter, buy a gag gift or perhaps take home a device to help them act out some formerly repressed sexual whim. Unlike the porn palaces in the sleazier sections of town which sell celluloid and literary fantasies, the Pleasure Chest offers the opportunity to make these dreams come true. Perpetual orgasm, kinky bliss and every other sensation described in the Penthouse Forum are here for the taking, provided you have ready money, or acceptable credit cards.

The first Pleasure Chest opened in New York in 1971 as a toy shop for gays. Four years later the Philadelphia branch opened its doors. Unlike the prosperous Manhattan original, the shop in the City of Brotherly Love specialized in red ink accounting.

Were Penn's gays more discriminating or merely less affluent? The owner didn't care to meditate on this puzzle. In an attempt to attract bourgeois customers, he moved his shop to the high-rent district around Rittenhouse Square, and switched to low-profile marketing techniques amid plush decor.

More and more family type folks with discretionary income came in to case the joint, and returned to suburbia laden with vibrators, dildoes and the leather ready-to-wear that represented the state-of-the-art in sexual chic. Out-of-state regulars from spots as distant as Maine and West Virginia drove in weekly to stock up on supplies. More visitors than you think come to the city of Brotherly Love to indulge their penchant for cruelty.

From the exterior the shop looks nondescript. No flashing neon lights. Not even one teensy X. The western window display is similar to the decor in the optical shops around the corner. Red padded satin lips and rings honor St. Valentine. The rings in the opticians' windows are hooked together, fit on the nose and improve the vision of the wearer. The rings in the Pleasure Chest window clip to leather bands and embrace another protruberance with hopefully an equally beneficial effect.

The eastern window is hidden by high stairs, and is the more depraved. Anal-ease and a Hot Shot (a colonic device that attaches to a faucet) are displayed amid erection cremes and less exotic unctions and ointments.

Lush foilage guards the interior view from the casual gaze of passersby. What's the store really like? Could an average middle-aged traditional mother view its wares without feeling outraged?

Sure. I'm an average, middle-aged traditional mother and I spent last Saturday afternoon at the Pleasure Chest as a sales trainee.

*

The Pleasure Chest opens at noon and by 12:02, a dozen shoppers were already milling around. Clean, well-dressed couples with bags from Bonwit Teller's. A pair of art lovers was fascinated by the current *chef-d'oeuvre* in the art gallery beside the entrance—a hand-sewn padded coverlet, list price 1,040 dollars, which can only be described as a fucking quilt. In the opposite alcove hung a Pleasure Swing which supplied a new use for remaindered isometric exercise kits. Designed to encourage midair coupling, at 40 bucks a crack, no one had yet been tempted to fly united.

Genital stimulators fill shelves in the center of the store. The Prelude 3 is the Rolls Royce of the line. Designed for clitoral stimulation (rather than insertion) and totally silent, the Prelude 3 is made to order for anyone who needs to climax without waking the children. I was told that women freaked out over the Prelude 3. Usually the buyer returns with a few friends in tow who've tried hers, loved it and come in to buy one of their very own. My housekeeping standards are very low, but I hope somebody took the Rolls to the carwash before passing it on to the next driver.

There's a basket filled with comic books, circa 1935, that present a new perspective into the daily activities of Maggie and Jiggs. Frilly lingerie, exactly like Frederick's of Hollywood, fills a bilevel rack. Fringe. Lace. Satin. Lots and lots of elastic. One size fits all, but I'm sure the black lace bras with those unsewed tips look more seductive on a 36C than they do on a 48 long.

The book department only offers operational manuals. *The Aphrodisiac Cookbook. The Complete Enema Guide.* How complete is complete? Over 100 pages. Pure overkill. I spent my childhood escaping from those red rubber bags and I can assure you that five simple words cover the entire subject in depth. Feets, don't fail me now!

Gay greeting cards show the Statue of Liberty in drag clothes and proclaim: "Not everybody wants to be a

Marine." The card rack guards the entrance to Nightmare Alley where the bondage equipment is pinned to the walls. A behemoth strides up and down the aisle comparing blind-folds, paddles and whips. Nothing else comes in his size.

Clerking wasn't difficult. People knew exactly what they wanted. Several men asked for their correspondence. The Pleasure Chest runs a post office for letters you don't want delivered at home. Giggling undergraduates stocked up on penis shaped pencil erasers, and one clean Nordic type bought a cheap vibrator. The manager inserted batteries in it to make sure it worked properly. Every device is tested before it gets wrapped and everything in the store is sold with a one year unconditional guarantee. There are no fit-ting rooms in the back for rather obvious reasons. The moaning and groaning from the rear could unnerve the uncommitted.

I wrote up all the sales and checked prices in the catalog. What really upset me most was computing the state sales tax from those tiny little figures taped to the bottom of the metal sales slip holder. I had left my reading glasses at home and I cheated Governer Thornberg out of 12 cents before I began to squint. I took cash. I gave change. I inserted the purchases into black bags with no store markings. The Pleasure Chest selects their wrappings to give their clients anonymity . . . but not from each other.

Two gays played with an undulating penis and told me their former roommate had struck it rich. Stosh had been selected to pose as a *Playgirl* centerfold.

"Can you imagine what he'll tell them for the write-up. About his sexual preferences, I mean . . ." simpered the taller one.

"He'll say what they all say," the younger one replied.

"That he adored Judy Garland, Jayne Mansfield, and Marilyn Monroe."

"Why?" I asked. "Does Stosh like beautiful show business types?"

"No," I was told. "He prefers women who are dead."

The two queens were displaced by the Hulk who lumbered up to the counter to discuss specifications. I was hardly the person to supply them. I request anesthesia even when having my teeth cleaned.

He and the manager evaluated the pros and cons of various restraints and blindfolds. After considerable deliberation the customer made his final selection—a studded paddle, a small black whip and a sturdy sheepskin blindfold. The set of adjustable nipple presses lying beside them clearly labeled the buyer as a novice. (The diehards prefer sooper-dooper alligator clamps.) A square of studded leather, really Greek to me, completed the order. It was a gauntlet and cost 50 cents per square inch.

While I added up his bill, the Hulk made a last minute impulse purchase. An irresistible vibrating cock ring raised his total to 104 dollars. He reached into the pockets of his leviathan jogging suit and pulled out several fresh, clean bills. After I put them in the till, I looked around for a giant size bag, but the Pleasure Chest wrapping supplies were clearly meant for smaller orders. I inserted the paddle obliquely into the largest bag, but he still walked out on Walnut Street with the handle in full view.

Another polite, clean gentleman bought a peculiar leather harness. I overcharged him. The cock ring that he selected should have been included in the harness price. An executive-type woman picked up a pair of handcuffs. They both paid with Mastercharge. They waited patiently until the amounts were authorized by the main office, thanked me politely and left.

I couldn't believe that these sweet souls would be using our stock to maul their near and dear. Maybe they just donned the purchases themselves and strutted around in front of a mirror. I took everything with a grain of salt, until, while zipping through the catalog to check some prices, I came across a page of gags that stood my hair on end. A few pages later, a group of anal inserters transformed my straight hair back into Shirley Temple ringlets.

What! No iron maidens? Maybe in 1981, if the owners could find an available moonlighting spikesmith. My psychosexual ruminations were cut short by a sudden wave of shoppers.

Two hours later I was totally bored. Retailing is very tedious work. Smiling is *de rigueur*. Given my druthers of sales establishments, I'd prefer a first-class gourmet shop.

Can people find pleasure in so much pain? I find that hard to believe, but just in case my imagination is limited I plan to speak to my investment counselor about the wisdom of selling my shares of I.B.M. and stocking up on rubber tubing.

Do the unctions and ointments really cure impotence? The owner insists they do. "China Brush" is an erection potion distilled in the mysterious Orient. The ingredients? All written out in Chinese calligraphy. Take the box to your laundryman for decoding. Have the Red Chinese come up with a truly ingenious use for all that leftover starch?

The owner took umbrage at my remark that his dildoes were overpriced. I was told that the prices in the shops in Hooker Heights were double those of the Pleasure Chest list.

The following day I drove down to Sleazeville, Pa. on a comparison shopping junket. I was not so idiotic as to visit The Strip unchaperoned. Guarding me was my luncheon companion, Baron Pottstown, the article muse. Baron lifts weights three evenings a week. His biceps are astounding. I was certain that the sight of his bulging muscles would protect me from possible abuse.

Our first stop, the Denmark Sexual Cinema, sported a solid neon facade. I looked through a stained-glass window in the storm door and saw a room that resembled a giant cigar box. Philippine mahogany panels with racks on racks of smut. A row of booths that showed sexual serials—25 cents for three minute's worth of film art with more plot than characterization.

As soon as I stepped through the doorway, depictions of lust assaulted my retinas from every conceivable angle. Three seedy men waited in line to convert their bills to silver.

The dildoes were encased in plastic envelopes and were displayed in the rear of the shop. I walked past the change brigade with my trusty notebook in hand. My praetorian guard? At the front of the store. His mind was not on his mission. We'd been cleft in twain by a reel of film that showed a Roman orgy.

A gutteral voice whispered to me, "Lady, you want to watch a movie?"

"No!" I screamed and dashed for the door, pulling Baron in tow. I never got a chance to check the prices. No matter what the Pleasure Chest charges, I'll buy my sex aids there. Dignity counts a lot when you're 46. Treated like a quarter whore, indeed! What average traditional middle-aged Mom could endure so great an insult?

Why do shops like this flourish? Americans have too much faith in the printed word. They regard the letters in *Hustler* and *Oui* as gospel rather than fiction. We're so success oriented that even love is graded. We have to keep up with the Joneses sexually as well as socially.

For most of us acting out fantasies is painful or disappointing. Underneath those tough facades we're all really shopping for love. Instead of coming on for our peers and buying paraphernalia, we'd be better off learning to operate our true sexual organ—the brain.

The Fucking School
Drop-Outs

When Alvin and I got married, one conviction united us. We both agreed that I was a very lucky woman to have hooked him for my mate. Alvin was affluent, successful and muscular. I was domineering, aggressive and plump. We were both equally overweight, yet the adjectives with the negative connotations always applied to me.

To tell the truth, Alvin was reluctant to tie the knot. I hounded him until he surrendered. His decision was practical rather than romantic. He thought I would make a good mother, I was a terrific cook, and I was too frightened of losing him to make real emotional demands.

The presumption that he was more special than I pervaded our lives in every way. Sexually, too. I didn't turn him on, so I had to be the aggressor. I felt lucky to get fucked. He convinced me I was unattractive.

With time and therapy I became more brave. My negative conditioning vanished, and I began to buck the system. I started to make demands. I resented being considered the inferior partner when I often suspected that just the opposite was true. Sexually, too, I was bored with being the one who did all the work. My feelings of dissatisfaction were compounded when a friend gave me *The Joy of Sex* as a Christmas gift. I am a true believer and I wanted those "loving" pictures in the book to be repeated in my bed.

"I don't want to be fucked any more," I blurted out right

after Christmas. "I want to be loved. I deserve it. I made your life wonderful."

Alvin reacted to the mere suggestion that he might not be super-marvy, as he always does, with howls of rage followed by threats of divorce. "No one else ever complained about me," he hissed.

"They were all after your money," I hissed back.

"If you don't like the way I am, you don't have to live here . . . " he mumbled.

The ultimate threat. Funny. It no longer scared me.

Alvin didn't understand why I was suddenly bugging him. I didn't realize either the origin of one of the bases of my discontent. My annual depression had just begun. The anniversary of my father's death was approaching. Perhaps because he and I were not close, I feel so bad at that time. Bogged down in filial guilt, I always make trouble for myself by January fifteenth. This year was no exception. I had decided that our marriage was a vast emotional wasteland in addition to being a sexual Sahara.

"What do you want that you don't have?" Alvin finally wailed. He's an outer-directed man who solves all problems with purchases.

I showed him several pages in *The Joy of Sex*. "I want equality!" I cried. It would do for starters.

He told me I was acting infantile. I really showed him how infantile I was . . . by brooding and sulking for a week. We barely said, "Hello."

Our son, Steven, took advantage of our estrangement. Whenever Alvi and I think it's Splitsville we both try to seduce the kid. Steven is no fool. He knows he's the spoils of war. His price is high.

He made the most of my fear that he'll end up as emo-

tionally constipated as his role model and dragged me to the
Video Palace to examine the latest Atari cartridges for his
TV games. (I only bought him three.) He knows only too
well that for Alvin shopping is the ultimate distraction and
he took him on a tour of the Radio Shack's household computer division.

When I care about Alvin I feed him fish and alfalfa
sprouts. When I'm angry at him, out comes the heavy
cream. I have always preferred widow's weeds to support
hearings. Haut cuisine never sent anybody to the electric
chair. Butterfat, the scourge of millions, has done in more
husbands than the bubonic plague. It might take a while,
but I got off to a good start. I suddenly found myself cooking the most marvelous gourmet meals. For one.

"More hollandaise, Alvin?"

"Just a drop."

"Can I have some hollandaise too?"

"I just made enough for your father."

"Triple chocolate or Piña Colada cheesecake, Alvin?"

"Could I have a sliver of both?"

"Sure," I replied and covered his plate with a giant dose
of artery cloggers.

"Why am I eating melon?" Steven would ask. "Why
won't you give me anything good?"

"Because it's not healthy. Do you want to get angina
when you get older or die of a heart attack?"

Alvin and I managed to be civil on the first floor, but our
bedroom became a real Antarctica. I really dislike living in
deep freeze, and I reviewed several methods of resolving our
differences. Psychotherapy was out. Alvin was not receptive
to introspection. It was impossible to get to his penis
through his head. Perhaps I might take the scenic route and

try to get to his head through his penis. Some friends of mine had reported significant emotional breakthroughs with a Masters and Johnson approach. After two weeks of celibacy, I suggested we give it a try.

Alvin mulled the idea over briefly. He didn't think it was necessary, but he would go with me if I made an appointment. He didn't want me to be unhappy.

I called a sex clinic at a nearby university for an appointment. I grew up with the dictum that the best always costs the most. A session with the department head was only 40 dollars an hour more. Well worth it, to save my brains from the ineptitude of trainees.

The first appointment we could get was a month away. I told them to book it for us. I'd have a little time to try to soften Alvin up at home. I wasn't dragging Alvin to a sex clinic just to indulge my genitals. Our relationship was a microcosm. The lack of communication between us merely reflected his general isolation from humanity. I wanted him to be loving and connect with many people, not just with me. Even a sexual fascist, as I am, likes to believe that her motives are pure.

The day before our first appointment, a blizzard hit the area. Fourteen inches of snow. Howling winds. Freezing temperatures. Did Alvin and I snuggle up together before a cozy fire? Not on your life. He made me dress in thermals and dragged me out into the storm. We trudged through drifts and across ice fields until we arrived at the subway entrance. At the end of the line we waited for hours to board a bus to the end of the line.

Alvin's partners were mixing a "demo" tape they had recorded for a singing group. I don't know why Alvin felt compelled to join them at the studio. He can't tell a C from

F sharp. We boogied until the sun went down. Public transportation wasn't running. We hitchhiked home and got a lift in a broken down truck that had no snow tires and slid all over the icy roads. It was a miracle that we weren't killed.

The following morning, the day of our appointment, the sun was shining, the snow was melting and all the major roads had been cleared. Alvin refused to use our car, because the driving conditions were too hazardous.

"There's no sense in going at all today. Those doctors all live in the suburbs. It's a waste of time to drag all the way out to West Philadelphia for nothing?" he argued.

All the way to West Philadelphia! It was only five miles away. Why hadn't Alvin worried about hazardous road conditions when he dragged me out to the northern suburbs in the midst of a raging blizzard?

I called the clinic to find out if they were open. The doctor was indeed in. Our appointment was scheduled for 1:30 but the secretary asked us to arrive a few minutes earlier, so that we would have time to fill out some forms.

Alvin told me we'd have to travel by bus. Did he plan to go in his robe? He showed no sign of getting dressed. He read his *New York Times*, talked on the telephone, did his push-ups and finally stepped into the shower.

In order to arrive at the clinic in time, because we were taking public transportation, we would have to leave our house no later than 12:30. Alvin didn't finish shaving until 12:35.

"Why are you acting so frantic?" he asked angrily. "Do you have to be a monomaniac about this too? We have plenty of time. The bus stop is around the corner."

The bus stop was five blocks from our door, and Alvin

was in no hurry to get there. Instead of racing down the
street as he usually does, he took baby steps. He examined
every window he passed and discussed the seams on his
shearling coat with a Vietnamese shoemaker who spoke
almost no English.

A number 42 bus waited at the corner, but Alvin refused
to board it. The D bus would let us off closer to the doctor's
office.

The next bus that stopped was also a 42 and so were the
five that followed. I hailed two cabs, but Alvin sent them
off. It was one of his days to be frugal.

When a D bus finally arrived at our corner, it was packed
to the gills with passengers. We squeezed into an empty spot
beside the driver and watched the bus move west at a snail's
pace, stopping for every single red light. I'm a fanatic about
promptness and I was getting more and more frantic.

When we stepped off the bus I didn't even bother to look
at my watch. I looked in my handbag for the appointment
slip with the doctor's address on it. I had left it at home. My
initial guess about the street number was wrong and Alvin
and I had to circumnavigate the block to get to the clinic. I
usually remember addresses. Why had I forgotten this one?
Maybe I wasn't so anxious to face this problem either.

Alvin made a few nasty comments. I replied in kind. The
closer we got to the therapist's office, the louder our screams
became.

"It's all your fault we're late," Alvin shouted. "If you'd
brought the appointment card, we wouldn't be wandering
around like a tribe of nomads!"

"We're late because you don't want to go at all! If you
weren't such a tightwad, we could have grabbed a cab and
been here an hour ago."

"Try working for money sometimes like I do. Maybe then you won't throw it around like a drunken sailor!" Alvin whirled around and waved an accusing finger in the air. "You think you know it all. Well, let me tell you, you don't! I'm not holding anything back this time. I'm going to tell this doctor EVERYTHING!"

Alvin's revelation really took me aback. Was there something awful about me that he had never revealed to anyone before? Oh, my God! I didn't want to hear anything awful about myself. We could still forget the whole thing. Let him remain an anal retentive and let me keep my illusions.

Alvin saw the fear in my face. He pressed forward to gain a greater advantage.

I couldn't give any quarter no matter what the consequences might be. "Fuck yourself with a blowtorch," I replied in his native tongue. Nothing was going the way I had planned. Selecting an impartial therapist instead of my good old loving shrink had obviously been a gross error in judgment on my part.

I was on the verge of tears. We were wasting time and money. Not even a wonder working Rabbi could put such a rotten marriage back together again.

No one cared that we were 20 minutes late. The people who had the appointment after us had been snowed in. We were each handed a clipboard with questionaires attached. The first one was designed to pinpoint areas of conflict in our marriage. Out of 73 possible trouble spots, Alvin and I only found two that caused us grief. We both began to smile. Maybe our relationship wasn't as awful as it had sounded on Walnut Street.

The second form contained a series of multiple choice

questions about our self-esteem. Depressions? We rarely
entertained them. We're both more murderous than
suicidal. We both had problems with this test because the
superlatives were understated. None of them accurately
described our feeling of self-love.

The doctor was glancing at our answers when we walked
into his office. He looked up at us with a confused expression. Why we were coming to him for treatment? I waited
nervously for Alvin to tell him everything. Does a leopard
change his spots? Alvin told the usual nothing.

He mentioned that young girls turn him on more than I
do, but he doesn't get involved with them, because he finds
our marriage pleasing in every other way. My complaints
about him focused on his emotional detachment. "He's too
passive sexually to suit me any more," I announced.

Alvin's moustache was bristling.

Before he could tell EVERYTHING, I blurted out our
secret. "He doesn't like the way I smell." After that it was a
piece of cake. I treated the doctor to a condensed version of
my analysis and summed up Alvin's less successful therapy
and his latent Oedipal hangups. When I smiled at the doctor, he smiled back. Perhaps he and I could work on Alvin's
problems as co-therapists.

"Are these reactions to yourself really accurate?" the
doctor asked.

"No," I admitted. "I really think I'm even more terrific."

"I don't get patients like you very often," he told us.
"Most people who come to me have real problems with self-
esteem. The sexual dysfunction is just one symptom of their
negative feelings about themselves."

"That's interesting," Alvin lied.

We were there because of problems with self-esteem, too.

I no longer had any problems with mine, and I was unwilling to be blamed for the deficiencies in our relationship. I waited for the doctor to tell Alvin that I was brilliant and absolutely marvelous, and that Alvin should cut out his shit and do whatever I said.

Instead he and Alvin traded platitudes. Alvin said he wanted me to be happy. The doctor was thrilled to hear that. I suspected Alvin was giving him a first class snow job. Were they both sexist pigs?

The doctor asked if Alvin wanted to try the program. Alvin repeated he was there to make me happy, and he would do whatever I wanted. He flashed his good little boy smile at Dr. Putz. Putz-o smiled right back. He obviously empathized with my poor husband. Living with an aggressive bitch like me was certainly no bed of roses.

The doctor walked over to the film library to pick up the first reel and returned empty handed. Lesson One had disappeared. He thought we could handle more advanced techniques and took Lesson Two from the shelf. He threaded the film into the projector, switched it on and discretely left the room. I tried to sit in Alvin's lap, but he pushed me off. He'll be right back," he whispered. Mr. Uptight. I sat in my chair. Alvin sat in his. We watched two very clean Wasps from Terre Haute talk for 15 minutes about rubbing each other. I found it hard to concentrate on their conversation. I just kept thinking about the four ounces of good caviar I could have bought with the money I was wasting on this visit.

The final third of the film showed the couple naked in bed. They rubbed and talked, but showed no feelings at all. They didn't embrace. They didn't neck. This wasn't where it was at for me. Alvin would have learned more about my desires by watching the courtship of Scarlett O'Hara in *Gone With the Wind*. I didn't want Alvin to give me a backrub. I wanted him to turn into Rhett Butler.

When the film was over, the doctor gave us our homework assignment. We were to imitate the rubbing techniques in the film. Any other love play was out. He also remarked that sometimes men resent being pushed, and that I should wait for Alvin to make the first move. I agreed to try, but I wasn't sure I had that much patience.

When I'm not a doubting Thomas, I am a true believer. Maybe I was too demanding. I'd try it the doctor's way. I went shopping for sensous oils and didn't find any I liked at Rite-Aid. While I was buying bran at the health food store, I noticed some oils that contained Vitamins A and E. Why not use a potion that might eliminate age spots, too?

I put the bottle on Alvin's night table. Not only did he ignore its presence, but he covered it later that night with a dirty handkerchief. A week went by. I waited in vain for a sexual advance from Alvin. Two days before we were due back at the clinic, he got around to it.

"I haven't had much of a sex urge," he apologized.

"I've noticed that, but you don't need a sex urge to massage me," I replied. "We aren't supposed to fuck."

"He didn't say that," Alvin insisted.

"Weren't you there in the room the entire hour?"

"Sure, but I don't remember him saying anything like that."

Was Alvin getting senile or had he merely taken advantage of the quiet in the doctor's office for a mental review of some of the tax shelters he'd been investigating. "It would be nice if you could manage to coordinate your head and body and brains."

"I'm just as together as you are," he snapped and stormed

out of the room. I heard the clang of steel striking against steel. The door slammed. Alvin was going into the night with his dearest friend. The world's dumbest dog. Spot.

That night we slept on opposite edges of the bed. Instead of bringing us together, sex therapy was polarizing our marriage even more.

The following day I arranged for Steven to sleep at a friend's house, so we could have time to do our homework in peace. I dressed my body up in a new, black, slinky nightgown—Wanamaker's Basement ($3.98). At that price it didn't matter if the oil stained it. Maybe Alvin would even be moved to rip the rag right off me. I put a casette of reggae music into the tape recorder. Alvin finds it sexy. I was going to give Masters and Johnson my all. I understood that the purpose of the massage was to improve sexual communication between us. As we pleasured each other we were supposed to reveal which zones were the most erogenous.

It was understood that I would rub first. Alvin disrobed and lay down prone on the bed. While I poured a drop of oil into my palm, Alvin announced, "You know I hate massages!"

After that, it was difficult, even for me, to be very optimistic.

Alvin hated giving massages even more than he disliked receiving them. In five seconds he had smeared oil all over me (front and back), and had turned over and gone to sleep. While I tossed and turned I worked on the progress report I would give that morning to Dr. Putz.

The doctor seemed pleased to see us. At least we didn't whine, like most of his patients. The smile remained on his face until I told him we had flunked massage—an omen of disaster.

"People who don't succeed in this part of the program

usually don't do well with the rest," he said sadly. He discussed sexuality with Alvin and gave him a suggested reading list. Why did Alvin look so fascinated? We both know he only reads thrillers. Was this saint sitting opposite me the same resistant man who shares my bed? Either I was married to a Dr. Jekyll and Mr. Hyde or Alvin deserved an Oscar for his performance.

"Do you want to see the next reel?" the doctor asked.

Both of us nodded yes. Maybe this time they'd show excerpts from Alvin's favorite, *Beyond the Green Door*.

No soap. That same Indiana couple demonstrated more extensive rubbing. That session *I* mentally reviewed the tax shelters.

The next day I dumped the A and E oil into the toilet and canceled our upcoming appointment. I was more qualified to handle Alvin's idiosyncrasies than a psychosexual fish.

The following week a story of mine was published in a literary journal. The imperfections in our coitus took second fiddle to that coup. Our sex lives changed more as a result of that short story than out of any insights we gleaned from our sessions of massage.

Alvin's perception of me changed dramatically. He became more vocal about his feelings and displayed more tenderness for me. So for the nonce I am content.

At this point in time, the intensity of my conversations is more important to me than the quality of my orgasms. So we're not always sexually perfect. Right now, who gives a damn? We've been together through thick and thin, and we like each other most of the time. When the ides of January draw nigh, it's a slightly different saga.

When I wallow in guilt about my father, my dissatisfactions are intensified. I think it would be divine to have a lover like Rhett Butler around. As a matter of fact, I had a lover once whose *raison d'étre* was my sexual satisfaction. I lived with him for 13 months, complaining bitterly all the time. Those wonderful orgasms came with one drawback. Occasionally I had to talk to him about something after the foreplay.

Having it Both Ways

I have always had a low bullshit tolerance and have never been receptive to dogma. That's one of the reasons I was a failure at the age of 30. Unmarried. College drop-out, (not once but THREE times). None of the jobs I ever held, billing typist (five years), prop hunter (two), were ever in the same league as my Stanford-Binet scores.

After I finally eked out a B.A. I became a long-term substitute in a ghetto school for a year and a half. To tell the truth, each day there seemed like a decade. I was flanked by educators who had majored in hall duty or earned doctorates in dicking around in the book closet. How could I cope with my position on the lowest rung of the educational totem pole, when in my heart I believed I deserved to be the ruler of the world? After I righteously reported several department heads who had asked me to teach their Latin classes during my free periods, fewer schools requested my presence.

My specialty then was living on the dole. I became an unemployment compensation expert and set a record during the '60's by receiving 75 checks in a row, with a brief seven week hiatus at the three-fifths mark while I lived off my income tax refund.

My poor Aunt Esther, a 62 year old senile dressmaker, and I signed for our first checks the very same week. Within a month, a job was found for that poor old lady who could no longer differentiate between a button and a needle. No suitable position was ever offered to me.

213

In those days, I reported to the office every Friday at 11:50 to sign for my check, supposedly prepared to go out on any job interview which the employment counselors might assign. Discussing employment possibilities with me would disrupt the staff's payday lunch plans, so I was sent out rarely on interviews. Just in case some overzealous placement advisor considered sacrificing her Friday martinis, I always appeared at the office in the same outrageous outfit—a stained tweed skirt (only one size too snug) paired with a shrunken pink turtleneck. They went together like fire and water. Neither make-up nor soap graced my face on Friday mornings. A bilious green kerchief concealed my uncombed locks. Moccasins and black nylons with a silver seam completed my costume. I verbalized a sincere desire to return to work as an administrative assistant. As the unsung innovator of *schlepper* chic I could have been hired as a fashion consultant to Janis Joplin.

When the checks ran out, some friends in the Women's Movement pushed me into applying for an executive position more commensurate with my IQ. I was hired to edit an Aerospace Journal by an engineer with the social graces of King Kong.

Was life at the top more satisfying? Not for me. I made more money but I was still taking instruction from inferiors. I hated working for others.

Some friends urged me to apply to Law School. Yuck! What in the world for? The lawyers I knew all zipped from state to state in airplanes, bearing briefcases filled with papers covered by archaic words. Spend my days defending thieves (great or petty) and killers (corporate or personal)? It did not turn me on.

The price for conventional success was too high. Going to the office every day was not for me. I believe that women are smarter than men and if working from nine to five was so terrific, we would have done it to begin with. To me, Eve's coup was not in getting Adam to bite the apple, but in convincing him that the five-day week was essential to his well-being. If stress was an aid to longevity, Fort Lauderdale would be filled with widowers instead of widows.

I knew I needed to be self-employed and marriage might be a better solution than the anxiety that accompanied the end of each course of compensation checks. Working for hire was awful enough, but job-hunting was positively degrading. I decided to depend on the love of a good man for my well-being rather than on the vagaries of the design department of the McDonnell Aircraft Corporation. Boarding collapsing DC-10's in the course of my employment was hardly my definition of pleasure.

I had long since cast off my mother's preaching. Stay a virgin and win a prince was not my philosophy. I auditioned men and found a perfect prospect. He was smart. He was fun. He loved making money and he was good at it. He was divorced and had no children.

His name was Alvin.

Alvin thought I would make a terrific wife and mother, but for someone else. That decision was far too crucial to my future to be left to his imperfect judgement. I didn't take no for an answer. I pursued him relentlessly and after 3 years of rejection wore him down. I accepted his impersonal proposal and have only lived to regret it 41 percent of the time. Alvin gets angry because I am philosophically incapable of stroking his ego, but I am a wonderful cook.

To celebrate our engagement I broke off all verbal communications with the Aerospace King Kong. I accepted his pay-checks but would not entertain his conversation. I had never found his temper tantrums very stimulating and armed with a two-carat diamond there was no reason for me to encourage them. In my employer's favor I must admit he was not a sexist pig. He treated both male and female staff members like shit.

Inviting him to my nuptuals would have been the same as inviting Hitler, so I didn't. In the mail on my morning as Mrs. Chanin, there was a billet-doux from my boss. He suspected I was planning to quit (I had no such intention) and was one-upping me by sending me a pink slip by special delivery.

Sacked on my first morning as a Mrs. made me into a legendary figure in the annals of the Jewish Princess. I have never worked for hire since. The gorilla had enclosed a $100 check as a wedding gift. He really did want love. He had given me an additional gift as well. I was once again eligible for unemployment compensation benefits. I filled out the application before we left for our New England honeymoon.

Until I got pregnant, six months later, I helped Alvin out at his law office. I just kept forgetting that he was the attorney and I was only the staff. It distressed me whenever his behavior differed from Clarence Darrow's. Alvin was involved with cash settlements. I represented the scales of justice.

On the sly I distributed petty cash to his starving clients only to discover that they were buying nickel bags instead of bowls of soup. Alvin was relieved when I took maternity leave and found other outlets for my ideals. He hired a real secretary who took dictation and lip.

Keeping a spotless house and raising perfect children was difficult work so I did neither. My mother had never permitted me to clean when I lived with her, as a result housekeeping implements and I were at odds. The roar of the vacuum cleaner upset my middle ear. My hands were congenitally unfitted to wield a mop. Once every fortnight, I strolled through our *pied-à-terre* with all my cleaning supplies—a roll of Scottowels and a spray bottle of Fantastik. Any surface, including carpets and couch, that looked deserving received the same remedy. A quick spritz and a fair-to-middling smearing.

My low housekeeping standards forced Alvin to steal the family housekeeper away from my sister-in-law. I fed her steaks and lobsters for lunch so she would never leave my side again. Relieved of household responsibilities, I devoted myself to opening charge accounts. It was swell to be welcomed with open arms by the same credit departments that had previously shunned me. My romance with possessions only lasted a few months. By the time my son Steven was a year old I was bored with consumerism. On to motherhood.

I felt an obligation to spend his formative years with my son. My housekeeper is a kind woman, but she does not share my motivation to make sure that Steven functions well when he is 30 years old. It was hard enough for me to battle his temper tantrums. Any sensible hired hand would surely choose to bribe him into pleasantness.

I wanted to have another child, so Steven could have a sibling. A shaky pregnancy was followed by a premature birth. That baby died 10 days later. I was deluged with guilt and refused to acknowledge my grief. I suddenly stopped ovulating and was unable to get pregnant again.

When the guilt caught up with me there was money for a good psychiatrist. One of the effects of my psychic delvings was a changed attitude toward my surroundings. I felt I deserved more pleasure than I was getting from life. Just because Alvin liked to squirrel away money was no reason for me to live in a dump. After battles that made Waterloo seem like child's play, Alvin engaged an architect. We moved into temporary quarters until the renovations on our house were complete.

During my period of dislocation, I lunched every day with the architect, Paul Vinicoff, later to become immortal as Baron Pottstown, the article muse. The restaurant we dined in served wonderful fish but rotten desserts. I convinced them to try my cheesecake. They loved it. Two months later I was MOTHER WONDERFUL™.

Out of my newly renovated kitchen, cardiac arresters poured. Alvin and I were not getting along. My baking business would supply me with income if my marriage broke up. I added clients and was delivering cheesecakes regularly to several of Philadelphia's finest dining rooms. I did enjoy controlling the taste buds of thousands. What oral fascist wouldn't?

I only used the richest and finest ingredients in my cakes. Most of the butterfat settled right on my hips. I was never comfortable baking in aprons or wiping my fingers on linen towels. In the MOTHER WONDERFUL kitchen batter was wiped from hands by human lips. Mine.

Once Alvin and I stabilized I bid my stove *adieu*. He didn't want me to give up a potentially lucrative business, but that did not deter me. Alvin made enough money for us to live on. It didn't make sense for me to look like Kate Smith so that Alvin could give more money to the feds.

We had just bought a fishing shack at the seashore with another couple. The kibbutz fantasy that spondored the purchase was quickly falling apart. I thought the story of our misadventures would make a funny book. I decided to try and write it. I had been an English major in college and the great white hope of the Temple University Creative Writing Department. It was time to try again.

Alvin treated my literary fantasy like another one of my whims. He saw stars right after he saw the bills that accompanied my start in the arts. I didn't slave in a garret with pencil stubs. I bought an IBM Selectric complete with service contract, sat it on a gorgeous white desk and inserted 25 percent rag bond. I sat my thinner ass on a Knoll secretarial chair and began to type away.

Even I was impressed with my true grit and my determination to pay my dues. I embraced those who would exploit me, and convinced them to put my name in print at any price. Granted there were days I wanted to jump out the window, like the morning I received five rejection slips, including one from *Kosher Home* (for a story that *Reader's Digest* eventually picked up). Delivering manuscripts on top of cheesecakes accelerated my acceptance rate. It even got me a cook-book offer from one publisher.

When a publisher with guts and imagination, Gloria Mosesson, took a chance on this book, I didn't have to argue about percentages. I accepted her offer because I appreciate her taking a chance on someone unknown and unusual and I want her to make an absolute fortune from this book. Me too. And if we don't I can try again without having to rewrite Erma Bombeck in order to make a fast buck.

I can appreciate the feminist demands of equal pay for equal work, but working for others is the road of the "good child" who can perform tasks that others praise. Staying home, tedious as that may appear to the executive woman, really suited someone as philosophical as me to a T. I'd rather have time to decipher my motivations than be financially independent. I'd rather make Alvin's breakfast and take the car to the shop than write annual reports and sit through meetings with corporate nerds.

As an artist I'm expected to be perverse. My reluctance to subscribe to whatever was "in" turned out to be my salvation. I took from tradition. I took from feminism. I was not trapped by either extreme. Instead I welded together two opposing points of view to enhance my coming of age. I don't have to worry about love or money. I just have to cope with Alvin's annual depression. That's much easier than coping with the ones I would be immersed in if I were working for IBM.

So here I am at 46 in my prime, with myself found and together. It would have been impossible without the sometimes reluctant support of the Jewish Prince who solved my financial problems when he walked down the aisle beside me. Do I tremble that Alvin will find some gorgeous mega-woman with enormous tits and say *Adieu* to me and aggravation? It could happen, but I think it's highly unlikely. We get along well, most of the time, and neither one of us is willing to give up our beautiful townhouse.

If I did one smart thing in life, it was to choose a mate who could afford to let me do my own thing. Every artist has a patron. My husband Alvin is mine.